What To Do With Your Life When You Have Indecision

14 Unconventional Lessons

Jake Morimoto

Table of Contents

Author's Note	2
Download for FREE: 60 Questions That Will Make You Instantly Smarter (+ a special bonus)	3
Introduction - Stop Asking "What Should I Do?"	7
1 - The Anti-Passion Manifesto	14
2 - Treat It Like a Buffet, Not a Soulmate	23
3 - Work Isn't Your Identity, and That's Liberating	38
4 - The Hobby That Saves You	48
5- Volunteer Like You Mean It	60
6 - The Beauty of Being Decent at a Lot of Things	70
7 - What Sports Can Teach You About Losing with Purpose	79
8 - Screw the Ladder – Build a Web	92
9 - Restlessness Is a Clue, Not a Curse	101
10 - What You Notice When You're Not Trying to Impress Anyone	111
11 - Being Average is Not an Insult	122
12 - The Inner Scorecard Revisited	131
13 - Don't Make a 10-Year Plan. Make a 10-Week Experiment	141
14 - You Don't Have to Be Useful All the Time	152
Conclusion: Maybe It's Not a Calling—Maybe It's Just a Life	162
A Tiny Favor That Would Mean the World to Me	169
My Next Book: What To Do With Your Life...When You're 40 and Still Unsure	170
Introduction: You're Not Late—You're Just Not Lying	173
1 - The Success You Wanted Then Might Be the Trap Now	180
My Other Books	188
Acknowledgments	191
About The Author	192
Bibliography	193

Copyright © 2025 by Jake Morimoto

All rights reserved. No part of this publication may be reproduced, distributed, or transmitted in any form or by any means, including photocopying, recording, or other electronic or mechanical methods, without the prior written permission of the publisher, except in the case of brief quotations embodied in critical reviews and certain other noncommercial uses permitted by copyright law.

For permission requests, contact hello@self-improvement.me

Published by Jake Morimoto

First Edition, 2025

Author's Note

This book is a collection of essays that forms part of the *Unconventional Wisdom* series.

You may notice that some essays draw on similar research or references. This is because they were originally written at different times as standalone pieces. When compiling this collection, I chose to preserve their original form for two reasons: first, the repetition reinforces key concepts central to the series; second, it allows readers the flexibility to dip into individual essays without needing to read the book cover to cover.

Whether you choose to read every essay or just a few, I hope you find something that resonates. Thank you for joining me on this journey, and I hope you enjoy the exploration.

JM

Download for FREE: 60 Questions That Will Make You Instantly Smarter (+ a special bonus)

Unlock a **FREE** exclusive **60 Unconventional Questions That Will Change Your Life** from the *Unconventional Wisdom* series!

What if the right question could unlock a better version of you?

This free, short book is packed with *60 sharp, surprising, and thought-provoking questions* designed to challenge how you think, spark powerful reflection, and change the way you see yourself and the world.

These aren't your typical self-help prompts; they're unconventional, provocative, and designed to make you smarter, clearer, and more future-ready.

Inside, you'll explore:

- Questions to Spark Deep Reflection
- Questions to Challenge Perspectives
- Questions to Uncover Hidden Knowledge
- Questions to Sharpen Thinking & Decision-Making
- Questions to Predict the Future Better
- Questions to Expand Your Perspective
- Questions to Become Smarter Through Others
- Questions to Deepen Relationships

Plus, as a bonus, you'll also get **free access** to the *Introduction* and *First Chapter* of my book:

How To Be Respected: 14 Unconventional Lessons on How You Earn Respect—and Keep It: an unfiltered, smart guide to earning lasting respect in a noisy, distracted world.

Get it now. It's free—and it might just change the way you think forever.

Just scan the QR code below (or go to <u>self-improvement.me/wh</u>) and get them now:

Introduction - Stop Asking "What Should I Do?"

You've been asking the wrong question this whole time.

"What should I do with my life?" It tumbles from desperate college graduates and haunts midlife crises. It wakes people at 3 AM and drives them to quit perfectly good jobs. It's scribbled in journals and whispered to therapists and shouted into the void of social media. This question has launched a thousand self-help books, career coaching seminars, and personality tests promising to decode your destiny.

And it's fundamentally broken.

When you ask "what should I do with my life," you're assuming there's a single correct answer waiting to be discovered—as if your purpose was predetermined and simply misplaced somewhere between childhood and adulthood. You're imagining that once found, this purpose will unfold in a neat, linear progression. You're expecting clarity to arrive in one magnificent epiphany, after which everything will finally make sense.

The uncomfortable truth? None of that is how life actually works.

I've spent years talking with people paralyzed by indecision—brilliant minds second-guessing themselves into stagnation, sensitive souls crushed by the weight of potential paths not taken. I've watched friends quit promising careers to "find themselves," only to discover that self-discovery doesn't pay the bills. I've witnessed the quiet desperation of those who believed they had found their calling, only to wake up one day feeling strangely empty despite checking all the right boxes.

Here's what nobody tells you: the "purpose" industrial complex doesn't exist to help you. It exists to sell you things. Courses. Books. Retreats. Solutions to a problem that has been deliberately oversimplified.

The philosopher Alain de Botton once observed that career anxiety is the price we pay for expecting work to deliver meaning in addition to money. In pre-industrial times, most people didn't choose their occupation—they inherited it. The blacksmith's son became a blacksmith. The question wasn't "what should I do?" but "how do I do this well?" Only in recent history have we developed the luxury—and the burden—of infinite choice combined with the expectation that our work should fulfill our deepest existential needs.

But what if purpose isn't something you find? What if it's something you build, gradually and imperfectly, through action rather than contemplation?

Derek Sivers, musician turned entrepreneur, built and sold CD Baby for $22 million through what he calls "accidental success"—a series of small helpful actions that accumulated into something significant, not a grand vision executed according to plan. His path wasn't linear; it was responsive.

He didn't follow a passion; he followed what worked, what interested him, and what seemed useful.

Modern culture has sold us a dangerous fantasy: that somewhere out there exists Our One True Calling, a perfect alignment of skill, passion, and market demand that will bring both fulfillment and financial security. We're told to "never settle" and that doing so means a life of quiet desperation. Meanwhile, the most interesting people I know have built lives by settling intelligently—not for less, but for specific constraints that foster creativity rather than endless, paralyzing options.

Charlie Munger, Warren Buffett's right-hand man and a brilliant polymath, advocates a "worldly wisdom" approach rather than narrow specialization. Instead of asking what single thing you should do, Munger would suggest building a "latticework of mental models"—becoming reasonably competent across multiple disciplines and finding value in the connections between them. The question shifts from "what's my purpose?" to "what problems are interesting to me, and what tools can I develop to solve them?"

You're not a brand. You're a human. Humans are messy, contradictory, and constantly evolving. We contain multitudes. We have seasons. We change our minds.

In 1997, psychologist Mihaly Csikszentmihalyi interviewed over 90 creative individuals who had made significant contributions to their fields. What he discovered wasn't a group of people who had followed a straight line to success, but rather individuals who remained exceptionally open to experience and willing to reinvent themselves repeatedly.

Their paths were marked by serendipity, side projects, and significant detours.

The world doesn't need more people desperately hunting for passion. It needs people willing to develop rare and valuable skills through the unglamorous process of deliberate practice. It needs people who understand that meaningful work often begins with simple curiosity rather than burning passion.

In a little-known study from 2002, researchers analyzed the career patterns of over 400 professionals and found that those who described themselves as "passionate" about their work rarely began that way. Most discovered their engagement through mastery—becoming good at something valuable led to autonomy, which led to purpose. Not the reverse.

Most of us will never have a single defining purpose. We'll have chapters. Phases. Projects. Experiments. Some will fail spectacularly. Others will succeed in ways we never anticipated. The most interesting lives rarely follow a script.

A ceramics teacher once divided her class into two groups. The first group would be graded solely on the quantity of work they produced—how many pots they could make. The second would be graded on quality—they needed to produce just one perfect pot. By semester's end, an interesting pattern emerged: the students graded on quantity were producing the highest quality work. While the "quality" group had spent months theorizing about perfection, the "quantity" group had been learning through iteration, failure, and practice.

Your life works the same way. The people who find fulfilling paths aren't those who think the hardest about what they should do. They're the ones who try things, who build skills, who engage with the world as it is rather than as they wish it to be.

The narrative of the "overnight success" obscures the years of seemingly unconnected experiences that often precede meaningful work. J.K. Rowling was a secretary, teacher, and researcher before Harry Potter. Before becoming the celebrated chef and owner of Momofuku, David Chang was studying religion, teaching English in Japan, and working as a telemarketer. Their paths make sense only in retrospect.

Our culture has romanticized the dramatic pivot—quitting everything to follow your dreams. We've fetishized the "leap of faith" narrative while ignoring the less dramatic but more reliable approach of building bridges between where you are and where you might want to go. Most successful transitions happen not through leaps but through intentional overlap—starting the new thing before completely abandoning the old.

Psychologist Gabriele Oettingen's research on positive thinking revealed a counterintuitive truth: those who only visualize success are actually less likely to achieve their goals than those who also contemplate obstacles. Dreams without practical constraints often remain dreams. The most effective goal-setting involves what Oettingen calls "mental contrasting"—imagining both the desired future and the challenges that stand in the way.

The question "what should I do with my life?" assumes that finding the right answer will dissolve your anxiety and set you on a clear path. But what if the anxiety itself isn't a problem to be solved but a natural response to being human in a complex world? What if the goal isn't to eliminate uncertainty but to build a healthy relationship with it?

Throughout this book, we'll explore alternatives to the broken question of purpose. We'll look at how to treat your career like a buffet rather than a soulmate, why being decent at many things might serve you better than excellence in one, and how cultivating seemingly useless hobbies might accidentally save your life. We'll examine why volunteering often breaks decision paralysis faster than introspection, how sports can teach us to lose with purpose, and why building a web of connections serves you better than climbing a ladder.

You'll meet people who found fulfillment not by chasing passion but by developing mastery, people who created hybrid careers that defy categorization, and people who learned to listen to their restlessness not as a curse but as valuable information. You'll discover why making 10-week experiments beats making 10-year plans, why being average at something you love is perfectly acceptable, and why sometimes the most productive thing you can do is absolutely nothing at all.

This isn't a roadmap to finding your purpose. It's an invitation to let go of that broken question and replace it with better ones. What problems do you find interesting? What skills could you develop that would be useful to others? What environments bring out your best? What can you contribute right now, even before you feel ready?

Maybe it's not a calling. Maybe it's just a life—beautiful in its incompleteness, meaningful not because of some grand design but because you choose to pay attention. Maybe the purpose isn't something you find but something you build, day by day, choice by choice, through work and rest and play and love.

Let's begin.

1 - The Anti-Passion Manifesto

There's a moment I've witnessed countless times. Someone stands at a crossroads in life—perhaps graduating college, leaving a job, or moving to a new city—and inevitably, a well-meaning friend or relative offers what has become our culture's most celebrated nugget of wisdom: "Just follow your passion."

This advice arrives with the weight of gospel truth. It's scribbled in graduation cards, emblazoned across Instagram posts, and preached from TED Talk stages. The message seems both irrefutable and simple: discover what you love, pursue it relentlessly, and fulfillment will naturally follow.

But what if this cornerstone of modern career guidance is fundamentally flawed?

The truth lurking beneath our passion-obsessed culture is far more nuanced than the inspirational posters suggest. For many people—perhaps most—the directive to "follow your passion" doesn't just miss the mark; it actively causes harm. It creates unrealistic expectations, fosters anxiety, and worst of all, sets up a false dichotomy that makes ordinary work feel like failure.

Let's be clear: I'm not advocating for a life of drudgery or suggesting you should settle for misery. Rather, I want to dismantle the modern mythology around passion and replace it with something more honest and ultimately more useful—a framework that acknowledges both how skills actually develop and how fulfillment genuinely emerges.

The inconvenient reality is that passion rarely precedes mastery. For most people, deep engagement and satisfaction grow gradually through the process of becoming good at something valuable. The causality runs backward from what we've been told: passion is more often the product of mastery, not its prerequisite.

Computer scientist Cal Newport explored this counterintuitive idea in his research on career satisfaction. After studying people with fulfilling careers, he discovered that very few began with a pre-existing passion that they simply pursued. Instead, they developed skills, gained competence, and through that process, cultivated a genuine love for their work. This perspective shift—from "follow your passion" to "develop rare and valuable skills"—fundamentally reorients how we might approach life's big decisions.

Consider the story of chef Brandon Baltzley, who began his culinary journey not out of some childhood dream or innate love of cooking, but as a dishwasher desperately needing a paycheck. Initially, food was merely the medium of his labor, not his passion. Yet through years of disciplined practice, attentiveness to craft, and gradual skill development, he eventually rose to become an acclaimed chef at several Michelin-starred restaurants. His passion for innovative cuisine emerged through mastery, not the other way around.

The narrative we tell ourselves matters profoundly. When we believe that we must first identify our singular passion before meaningful work can begin, we create a paralyzing pressure. Each career move feels like an existential commitment: Is this really my passion? What if I choose wrong? The anxiety this creates can lead to decision paralysis or, just as commonly, premature abandonment of promising paths before mastery has a chance to develop.

Life doesn't often announce its most fitting paths with trumpet blasts of immediate passion. More commonly, it whispers through quiet moments of satisfaction in work done well, through the subtle pleasure of solving problems, or through the gradual realization that you've developed an unusual perspective on something that matters.

Angela Duckworth's research on "grit"—the combination of passion and perseverance—offers another angle on this misconception. Her studies show that high achievers aren't necessarily those who felt an immediate calling to their field. Rather, they're often those who stuck with their endeavors long enough to reach the stage where intrinsic rewards begin to multiply. Perseverance often precedes passion, not the reverse.

Imagine standing before a locked door that you believe contains your future happiness. The "follow your passion" doctrine suggests you must first find the perfect key—your singular passion—before you can unlock a fulfilling life. But what if the reality is more akin to a locksmith slowly learning to craft keys through trial and error? The satisfaction comes not from finding some pre-existing

16

perfect match but through developing the skills to create what fits.

This alternative approach—developing rare and valuable skills first—offers several advantages over the passion-first model. It reduces the pressure of making perfect initial choices. It acknowledges that interests evolve and transform. Most importantly, it places agency back in your hands rather than leaving you waiting for a lightning bolt of passion to strike.

The quieter truth is that meaningful work often begins not with excitement but with curiosity, or sometimes mere convenience. These modest starting points are nothing to be ashamed of. They're the realistic soil from which sustainable careers actually grow.

In 1994, a computer programmer named Pierre Omidyar started building a simple auction website as a hobby project. It wasn't his lifelong passion—just an interesting coding challenge and potential small business. That modest beginning eventually became eBay. While the billion-dollar outcome is exceptional, the pattern is common: world-changing work often begins not with passion but with simple curiosity about solving an interesting problem.

Our culture's passion fixation has another insidious effect: it creates a hierarchy of work, elevating "passion careers" while implicitly devaluing everything else. This is both classist and disconnected from how satisfaction actually operates. Meaningful work exists across the spectrum of human endeavor, not just in a select few Instagram-friendly creative fields.

Mike Rowe, known for hosting "Dirty Jobs," has spent years documenting people who have found profound satisfaction in careers that most would never describe as "follow your passion" material. He tells the story of Les Swanson, a septic tank cleaner who built a successful business and takes immense pride in his expertise. Swanson didn't grow up dreaming of sewage systems, but through mastery and autonomy, he found satisfaction that many passion-followers still desperately seek.

The "follow your passion" narrative also carries an implicit assumption of privilege. It presumes you have the economic freedom to prioritize personal fulfillment over immediate income, the educational background to access passion-friendly industries, and the social capital to network your way in. For many people worldwide, these are luxuries beyond reach. A more universal approach to meaningful work must account for the realities of economic necessity.

The truth is that seemingly ordinary work, approached with curiosity and commitment, can yield extraordinary satisfaction. This satisfaction comes not necessarily from the nature of the task itself but from the autonomy, mastery, and purpose you cultivate within it. As psychologist Mihaly Csikszentmihalyi discovered in his research on "flow states," engagement and absorption can happen in almost any activity pursued with the right combination of challenge and skill.

I once spoke with a city bus driver who described the deep satisfaction he found in perfectly timing traffic lights, memorizing his regular passengers' habits, and finding small ways to make their commutes more pleasant. His passion wasn't for driving buses specifically—it emerged from mastering the subtle complexities of his role and recognizing its impact on others. This pattern repeats across fields: satisfaction grows from engagement and mastery rather than from the surface-level description of the work.

So what might a post-passion approach to finding your work look like? First, it means shifting your focus from identifying pre-existing passions to developing valuable skills. Ask not what you already love, but what you're willing to work at becoming exceptional at doing.

Second, it means embracing the apprenticeship phase of any endeavor. Too many people abandon promising paths before they've had time to develop the competence that makes work rewarding. Anticipate that the early stages of almost any worthwhile pursuit will involve confusion, frustration, and only glimpses of the satisfaction that comes with mastery.

Third, it means recognizing that motivation often follows action rather than preceding it. Beginning without passion doesn't mean you'll never find it—it often means you haven't yet developed the skills that make an activity intrinsically rewarding.

This approach also requires humility. The "follow your passion" doctrine contains an implicit grandiosity—the assumption that your work should constantly excite and fulfill you, that you're somehow entitled to perpetual engagement. Real work, even deeply satisfying work, includes mundane tasks, frustrations, and periods of doubt. Accepting this reality isn't settling; it's maturing.

Novelist Haruki Murakami provides an illuminating perspective on this process. Before becoming one of the world's most celebrated authors, he ran a jazz club. His transition to writing wasn't driven by some lifelong burning passion—it began with a simple moment at a baseball game when he suddenly thought, "I could write a novel." He started writing after work each night, driven not by passion but by curiosity about whether he could actually complete a book. Only through the disciplined act of writing did his love for the craft develop.

"In most cases, learning comes before passion, not the other way around," explains organizational psychologist Adam Grant. He points to research showing that interests typically develop after people gain competence in a field, not before. We've simply confused cause and effect in our cultural narrative about fulfilling work.

The anti-passion approach I'm advocating doesn't mean abandoning the search for satisfaction. It means recognizing that satisfaction typically comes through the back door of skill development rather than the front door of pre-existing passion. It means understanding that meaningful work is less about what you do and more about how you approach what you do.

Let me be clear about what this isn't: this isn't an argument for staying in truly miserable circumstances or for ignoring your genuine inclinations. It's about recognizing that the path to meaningful work is rarely as straightforward as "identify passion, then pursue it."

If you currently find yourself at a crossroads, paralyzed by the pressure to identify your one true calling, here's a liberating alternative: choose something that interests you moderately and that allows you to develop valuable skills. Commit to becoming genuinely good at it. Notice the subtle moments of engagement and satisfaction that emerge as your competence grows. Follow those moments rather than some abstract notion of passion.

Remember that your relationship with your work will evolve. What begins as a practical choice might develop into deep engagement as you master its complexities. What feels like a passionate calling may reveal significant downsides once the initial excitement fades. Either way, your capacity to find meaning comes not from the perfect initial choice but from your approach to the work itself.

The anti-passion manifesto, ultimately, is about liberation from the crushing pressure to immediately identify the perfect path. It's about recognizing that meaningful work emerges gradually through engagement, mastery, and connection—not through some magical moment of passion-discovery.

Perhaps most importantly, it's about honoring the dignity of all forms of work approached with craftsmanship and care, not just those few fields our culture has arbitrarily designated as passion-worthy. The satisfactions of competence, contribution, and craft are available across the spectrum of human endeavor, not just in a select few Instagram-friendly careers.

So the next time someone tells you to follow your passion, consider offering a gentle correction: "Actually, I'm planning to develop rare and valuable skills in something interesting, and I'll let passion find me through mastery." It's less quotable, certainly less Instagram-worthy, but infinitely more likely to lead you toward truly satisfying work.

2 - Treat It Like a Buffet, Not a Soulmate

They told you there's this perfect thing out there waiting to be discovered. A passion that will ignite your soul. A calling that will make Monday mornings feel like Christmas. A purpose so aligned with your essence that work and play become indistinguishable.

What a magnificent lie.

The cultural narrative of the "one true calling" is perhaps the most elegant trap we've built for ourselves in the modern age. It sounds spiritual. It sounds romantic. It sounds like destiny. And when we fail to find it—which most of us inevitably do—we assume the fault lies within us rather than with the premise itself.

Here's a more liberating truth: your relationship with work doesn't need to mirror a fairy tale romance. You don't need to search for "the one." Instead, imagine approaching your career path like a magnificent buffet spread before you—plentiful, varied, surprising, and offering multiple visits.

This essay isn't about lowering your standards or settling for mediocrity. It's about freeing yourself from the tyranny of singularity. It's about embracing the abundance of possibilities rather than the scarcity of perfection.

The mythology of the one true calling runs deep in our culture. We celebrate the violinist who knew from age four that music was her destiny. We admire the entrepreneur who built an empire around his childhood fascination with computers. We share quotes from luminaries who proclaim that once you find your passion, you'll "never work another day in your life."

These stories aren't necessarily false, but they represent statistical anomalies that we've elevated to normative expectations. It's like building your financial plan around winning the lottery—possible, but not probable. And worse, it creates a false binary: either you've found your magical calling, or you're failing at life's most fundamental quest.

Behind this narrative lurks a fundamental philosophical error—the assumption that we are static beings with fixed essences waiting to be discovered. As if we're born with a singular purpose encoded in our DNA, and life is merely the process of uncovering that hidden program.

The reality is far more fluid. Humans are constantly evolving, shaped by experience, learning, relationships, and circumstances. What resonates deeply at 25 may feel hollow at 35. The work that fulfills you during one life stage may suffocate you in another.

This stifling search for "the one" bears striking resemblance to another domain where we once insisted on singularity: romantic relationships. Just as our grandparents were expected to find their one soulmate and commit for life (regardless of growth or change), we now demand this same unwavering devotion to a singular career path.

But even relationships have evolved. Many thoughtful people now recognize that different partners might be right for different life stages. We acknowledge that love can take various forms and serve diverse purposes throughout our lives. Perhaps it's time we granted ourselves the same permission with our work.

Behavioral economists have documented what they call "the paradox of choice"—the counterintuitive finding that having too many options often leads to decision paralysis and reduced satisfaction. When faced with endless possibilities, we freeze, and whatever we ultimately choose feels inadequate compared to the idealized alternatives we rejected.

Barry Schwartz, who popularized this concept, distinguishes between two decision-making styles: "maximizers" who exhaustively search for the best possible option, and "satisficers" who select the first acceptable choice they encounter. His research consistently shows that while maximizers might achieve objectively better outcomes, satisficers report greater happiness with their decisions.

This finding hints at something profound about human psychology that applies directly to career choices. The relentless pursuit of the optimal path—the perfect match between your essence and your occupation—often yields diminishing returns of satisfaction. The burden of constantly wondering "what if" becomes heavier than the joy of what is.

But there's a less discussed flip side to this paradox—what researchers call "exploratory behavior." Animals, including humans, have built-in drives to sample various options before settling. This exploration serves an evolutionary purpose: it builds cognitive maps of our environment and expands our adaptability.

In one fascinating study at Northwestern University that received little mainstream attention, researchers found that people who engaged in "career sampling"—trying different professional paths before committing—reported higher job satisfaction in midlife than those who pursued linear trajectories. This finding contradicts the common wisdom that "finding your passion early" leads to greater fulfillment.

The researchers labeled this approach "the portfolio career strategy"—treating your professional life not as a single investment but as a diversified portfolio of experiences, skills, and identities. The psychological security that comes from this diversification allows for greater risk-taking and, paradoxically, deeper commitment to current projects.

I spoke with a former investment banker turned organic farmer who explained it this way: "Banking taught me discipline and financial literacy. Those weren't my passion, but they were valuable. Farming isn't my ultimate passion either—it's my current commitment. The difference is liberating."

Jazz legend Miles Davis once remarked, "Sometimes you have to play a long time to be able to play like yourself." His insight captures something essential about mastery and identity—they emerge through practice rather than precede it.

Our culture has inverted this wisdom, suggesting that we should first identify our authentic selves and then choose work that matches this pre-existing identity. But what if the relationship works in reverse? What if identity emerges from commitment rather than directing it?

This perspective aligns with the research of psychologist Dan McAdams, whose life-story model of identity suggests that our sense of self emerges primarily through the narratives we construct about our experiences after they occur. In other words, we don't find ourselves and then act accordingly; we act, and then make meaning of those actions to understand who we are becoming.

Consider the career trajectory of Temple Grandin, whose groundbreaking work in animal behavior and autism advocacy didn't emerge from a lightning bolt of purpose. Her path began with a series of specific problems she wanted to solve, many stemming from her own experiences with autism. Her sense of calling emerged gradually through engagement rather than revelation.

Or take the lesser-known example of Cleve Jones, a San Francisco activist who created the AIDS Memorial Quilt. Jones didn't set out with a grand vision of creating what would become the largest community art project in history.

He began by addressing immediate needs in his community during the AIDS crisis. The quilt—which now contains over 48,000 panels commemorating lives lost to AIDS—emerged organically from a specific act: posting placards with names of the dead on the San Francisco Federal Building during a march in 1985. Jones's purpose evolved through action, not preceding it.

The key insight here is that meaning often follows mastery rather than driving it. By treating your career as a buffet rather than a soulmate search, you grant yourself permission to sample, to develop competence in various domains, and to allow your sense of purpose to emerge through engagement rather than anticipate it.

If we reframe career development as exploration rather than discovery, entirely new possibilities emerge. The pressure to find "the one" gives way to curiosity about the many. The anxiety about making a wrong choice diminishes when we recognize that each professional experience—even those that don't ultimately become lifelong commitments—contributes valuable ingredients to our unique recipe.

This mindset shift has practical implications. Rather than asking the paralyzing question, "What is my passion?" we might ask more productive questions like: "What am I curious about right now?" "What problems do I find interesting?" "What environments bring out my best qualities?" "What skills would I like to develop next?"

These questions orient us toward action rather than introspection, toward sampling rather than committing prematurely.

The buffet metaphor extends further. At an actual buffet, we don't feel obligated to love everything we try. We sample, we discover preferences, we return for seconds of what delights us. Some dishes surprise us—flavors we didn't expect to enjoy become favorites. Others disappoint —options that looked appealing turn out to be less satisfying than anticipated.

But here's the crucial point: these discoveries happen through tasting, not through analyzing the menu. Similarly, career clarity emerges through experience, not endless introspection.

This approach aligns with what designer and computer scientist Bill Burnett calls "prototyping your life"—creating small, low-risk experiments to test different career elements before making major commitments. Informational interviews, volunteer projects, weekend workshops, online courses—these are all ways to sample the buffet without the pressure of choosing a single lifelong path.

The solopreneur movement provides particularly rich examples of the buffet approach in action. These independent professionals often create hybrid careers that combine multiple interests, skills, and revenue streams.

Rather than identifying with a single profession, they build portfolio careers that evolve organically over time.

Consider the case of Shannon, a former corporate attorney who grew increasingly dissatisfied with the disconnect between her daily work and her values. Rather than attempting to identify her "one true calling," Shannon began experimenting with side projects while maintaining her legal practice.

She started a small legal blog addressing environmental issues, which led to speaking engagements at sustainability conferences. These connections opened opportunities to provide legal consulting for conservation nonprofits. Eventually, she developed expertise in sustainable business practices, which evolved into a consulting practice helping companies implement environmentally responsible policies.

Today, Shannon's work combines elements of law, writing, speaking, teaching, and consulting. Asked if she's found her calling, she laughs: "I stopped looking for it. Instead, I just keep following what interests me and what seems useful. My work today combines pieces of everything I've done before, but I couldn't have planned this path if I tried."

Shannon's story illustrates what researchers call "planned happenstance"—the process by which curiosity, persistence, flexibility, optimism, and risk-taking allow people to generate and recognize opportunities that weren't previously visible. Rather than executing a predetermined plan based on a singular passion, Shannon remained open to emerging possibilities. She treated her career as a buffet to be sampled rather than a soulmate to be discovered.

This approach doesn't mean abandoning commitment. Quite the opposite—it enables more authentic commitment because it's based on actual experience rather than idealized projections. Shannon isn't less committed to her work because she arrived at it through exploration; she's more committed because her path emerged from genuine engagement rather than abstract notions of what should fulfill her.

The cultural mythology of the "one true calling" is particularly pernicious because it suggests that work should satisfy all our needs for meaning, identity, and purpose. It places an impossible burden on our careers to fulfill emotional and spiritual needs that historically were distributed across many domains of life.

This concentration of purpose in professional identity is a relatively recent development. Throughout most of human history, work was just one aspect of a multifaceted life, not the primary source of meaning and identity. People derived purpose from family roles, community engagement, religious practice, creative expression, and cultural traditions—not just occupational titles.

By treating your career as one important element of a well-lived life rather than its defining feature, you distribute the weight of meaning-making across multiple domains. Work becomes important without becoming everything.

This perspective aligns with research from the field of positive psychology on what constitutes a satisfying life. Martin Seligman's PERMA model identifies five components of well-being: Positive emotions, Engagement, Relationships, Meaning, and Accomplishment. Notably, these elements can be cultivated across various life domains, not exclusively through paid work.

The buffet approach extends beyond career to life design more broadly. Rather than seeking a single source of fulfillment, we might create a portfolio of meaningful engagements—some that provide financial security, others that offer creative expression, still others that foster deep connection or contribute to causes beyond ourselves.

Perhaps the most compelling evidence for the buffet approach comes from those who've lived long enough to reflect on entire careers rather than isolated segments. In a remarkable longitudinal study conducted through the Harvard Grant Study, researchers followed the lives of 268 Harvard graduates for over 75 years, documenting their professional trajectories, relationships, and life satisfaction.

One of the study's most striking findings was that career paths rarely unfolded as participants had anticipated in their twenties. Those who maintained rigid attachments to specific professional identities generally reported lower satisfaction than those who adapted their ambitions to changing circumstances and emerging interests.

George Vaillant, who directed the study for decades, noted that career satisfaction was more strongly correlated with the ability to adapt than with the achievement of specific professional goals. Those who thrived maintained what Vaillant called "both/and thinking"—the capacity to pursue excellence while remaining flexible about the form that excellence might take.

This finding echoes the perspective of psychologist John Krumboltz, who argued that "planned happenstance" is more valuable than rigid career planning in an unpredictable world. Krumboltz suggested that career counseling should focus less on matching personalities to professions and more on developing the adaptive skills needed to recognize and capitalize on unexpected opportunities.

If we abandon the search for "the one" in favor of thoughtful sampling, how do we avoid becoming dilettantes? How do we balance exploration with the depth that comes from sustained commitment?

The key lies in distinguishing between sampling and skimming. Effective sampling involves genuine engagement—developing sufficient competence to evaluate whether a particular path merits deeper investment. This requires what psychologist Carol Dweck calls a "growth mindset"—the belief that abilities can be developed through dedication and hard work.

With this perspective, trying different career paths isn't aimless wandering but intentional exploration. Each experience builds transferable skills and self-knowledge that inform future choices. The goal isn't to find the perfect match for some pre-existing passion but to engage fully enough with various options to discover what engages you.

This approach has been exemplified by what writer David Epstein calls "late specializers"—people who explore multiple domains before focusing their energies. In his research on top performers across various fields, Epstein found that those who sampled widely before specializing often developed more innovative approaches than those who specialized early.

Francis Ford Coppola, before directing The Godfather, studied theater, music, and engineering. Julia Child worked in advertising and government intelligence before discovering her passion for French cooking at age 36. Andrea Bocelli practiced law before fully committing to his operatic career in his thirties.

These "late specializers" didn't lack direction; they were gathering ingredients for uniquely integrated careers. Their diverse experiences became assets rather than detours.

The buffet approach also offers psychological protection against what psychologists call "identity foreclosure"—prematurely committing to an identity before adequately exploring alternatives. When we define ourselves too rigidly around a single professional identity, we become vulnerable to crisis if that identity is threatened by industry changes, health challenges, or evolving interests.

By contrast, those who maintain multiple sources of meaning and identity demonstrate greater resilience when facing career disruptions. Research on psychological resilience consistently shows that flexible self-concepts—identities that encompass multiple roles and capacities—buffer against depression and anxiety during major life transitions.

This flexibility doesn't imply a lack of commitment or depth. Rather, it suggests a more nuanced understanding of commitment—one that recognizes that sustained engagement with meaningful work can take various forms throughout a lifetime.

Perhaps the greatest gift of the buffet mindset is the permission it grants to change your mind—to acknowledge that growth often requires relinquishing former certainties. By treating your career as an evolving portfolio rather than a single fixed calling, you create space for continual realignment between your work and your developing self.

This perspective aligns with what psychologist Dan Gilbert calls "synthetic happiness"—the discovery that our capacity for fulfillment is more adaptable than we imagine. Gilbert's research suggests that we consistently overestimate how much specific outcomes will affect our happiness and underestimate our ability to find meaning in unexpected circumstances.

The implications for career development are profound. If we can find fulfillment across various paths rather than requiring one perfect match, the pressure to identify a singular passion diminishes. We become free to commit fully to our current work while remaining open to evolution.

This isn't an argument for aimless drifting or commitment phobia. Quite the opposite—it's an invitation to more authentic commitment based on experience rather than expectation. When we sample the buffet, we discover genuine preferences rather than inherited assumptions. We commit from a place of knowledge rather than hope.

The buffet mindset acknowledges a fundamental truth about human development: we don't just find ourselves; we create ourselves through the choices we make and the meaning we derive from them. Our professional identities aren't discovered fully formed; they're cultivated through engagement with the world.

So perhaps it's time to release the exhausting search for your one true calling. Instead, approach the magnificent buffet of possibilities before you with curiosity and courage. Sample widely but engage deeply. Develop mastery while maintaining flexibility. Build a portfolio rather than a single investment.

Your life's work isn't waiting to be discovered like a hidden treasure. It's emerging through your choices, your commitments, and your willingness to grow beyond who you've been. The buffet is abundant, and you're welcome to return as often as you like.

3 - Work Isn't Your Identity, and That's Liberating

The question arrives like clockwork at parties, networking events, and family gatherings: "So, what do you do?" Not who you are. Not what you love. Not what keeps you up at night wondering about the universe. What you *do*—meaning, how you earn money. The answer to this question has somehow become the shorthand for our entire existence.

We've been sold a peculiar idea: that our work should be our identity, our calling, our purpose, the center around which our life orbits. It's as if the business card we carry defines not just our income source but the very essence of who we are. Software engineer. Marketing director. Teacher. Doctor. Barista. Construction worker. Each title comes pre-loaded with assumptions about our intelligence, our worth, our place in society's hierarchy.

This fusion of identity and occupation is a relatively modern invention. Throughout most of human history, people worked to live, not lived to work. A medieval blacksmith might have taken pride in his craft, but he wouldn't have introduced himself as "Hi, I'm John, and I'm passionate about metallurgical transformation processes." He was John, who happened to be a blacksmith, but also a father, a community member, a person with interests beyond the forge.

Today's complete integration of identity and work isn't just conceptually flawed—it's actively harmful. When we believe our value comes primarily from our productive output, we set ourselves up for an existential crisis every time our work circumstances change. Retirement, job loss, career transitions, or simply the inevitable days when work feels meaningless all become threats not just to our income but to our very sense of self.

British philosopher Roman Krznaric calls this phenomenon "self-work fusion," noting how this mindset leaves us vulnerable to exploitation. We accept longer hours, intrusions into our personal time, and outrageous workplace demands because to push back would threaten not just our job but our identity. The company knows this too. How many corporate cultures emphasize being a "family" or having "passion for the mission" while simultaneously underpaying their employees? When work is your identity, saying no becomes nearly impossible.

This identity-work fusion explains why unemployment can be so psychologically devastating, far beyond the obvious financial stress. In his lesser-known work "The Unemployed Man and His Family," published in 1940, Austrian psychologist Paul Lazarsfeld documented how job loss creates not just economic hardship but a profound identity crisis. Men who lost their jobs during the Great Depression experienced what Lazarsfeld called "a shrinking personality"—they felt diminished as human beings, not just as workers.

Eight decades later, little has changed. A 2018 study in the Journal of Organizational Behavior found that unemployment affects identity far more negatively in countries with strong work-centered cultures. Americans and Japanese suffered more profound identity crises when unemployed than their counterparts in nations like France or Italy, where cultural life extends more robustly beyond the workplace.

The good news buried within this problem is that recognizing the trap is the first step toward liberation. Once you understand that you are not your job title, you can begin building a more resilient, multifaceted identity that no economic downturn, difficult boss, or career change can threaten.

There's something quietly revolutionary about introducing yourself without reference to your job. Try it sometime. When someone asks what you do, talk about your fascinating hobby restoring vintage motorcycles, or how you've been learning to play the cello, or your volunteer work at the community garden. Notice their confusion, the brief system error as they try to place you in the hierarchy without an occupational label. Now notice your own discomfort—the strange vulnerability of being seen as a whole person rather than a productive unit.

Perhaps the most profound liberation comes when we flip the script entirely: your work doesn't need to express who you are. Instead, who you are—your values, your humanity, your unique perspective—can inform how you approach your work, whatever that work may be.

40

Take the story of Daryl Davis, a Black musician who has spent decades befriending members of the Ku Klux Klan, helping many to renounce their racism. Davis doesn't define himself by his day job playing piano. Rather, his deep-seated values of compassion and dialogue shape how he moves through the world, including in his music career. When asked why he reaches out to people who hate him because of his skin color, Davis simply says, "When two enemies are talking, they're not fighting." His work is an expression of his values, not the source of his identity.

The overidentification with productivity runs particularly deep in American culture, where the Protestant work ethic morphed into what sociologist Max Weber called the "spirit of capitalism." Weber observed how religious notions of calling and divine purpose gradually transformed into secular obsessions with career advancement and material success. The religious concept that work could be a form of worship became twisted into the idea that work itself was worthy of worship.

This mindset creates what philosopher Byung-Chul Han calls the "achievement society" in his book "The Burnout Society." We've internalized the demand to be constantly productive to such a degree that we've become our own taskmasters. "The achievement-subject exploits itself until it burns out," Han writes. We've replaced external exploitation with willing self-exploitation, all in service of an identity built around productivity.

A few years ago, I encountered an electrician named Miguel who embodied a different approach. When I complimented his work rewiring my home, he smiled and said, "I do good work because I respect the craft, but it's not who I am. I'm a grandfather first, a community organizer second, and the guy who makes sure your lights turn on third." Miguel worked with precision and care, but he never confused his job with his identity. On weekends, he taught neighborhood kids about local history and ecology, knowledge passed down from his indigenous ancestors. His sense of self remained intact regardless of economic circumstances.

The pandemic forced many to confront this question directly. When lawyers, teachers, and executives suddenly found themselves on Zoom in sweatpants, caring for children between meetings, the artificial boundaries between "professional self" and "real self" collapsed. For some, this collapse was terrifying. For others, it was the first breath of fresh air they'd taken in decades.

A particularly powerful example comes from the world of professional sports, where identity and performance are deeply entwined. Spanish tennis player Rafael Nadal once explained his mental approach: "I'm not just a tennis player; I'm a person who plays tennis." This subtle distinction allowed him to maintain equilibrium through injuries and defeats that might have devastated someone whose entire self-concept was built around athletic achievement. When Nadal loses a match, he hasn't failed as a person—he's simply a person who didn't win that day.

Consider how differently we might approach career choices if we truly believed our work was just one facet of a complete life, rather than its defining feature. You might choose a stable, unexciting job that funds your true passions. You might take more risks, knowing a failed venture doesn't make you a failed human. You might prioritize work with flexible hours over prestigious titles, creating space for relationships and experiences that bring deeper fulfillment.

What's truly remarkable is how many people find profound satisfaction in so-called "ordinary" jobs precisely because they've separated identity from occupation. In Matthew Crawford's philosophical memoir "Shop Class as Soulcraft," he describes leaving a prestigious think tank job to open a motorcycle repair shop. Crawford found that working with his hands offered concrete satisfaction that abstract knowledge work lacked. The motorcycle mechanic knows when a job is done and done well. The policy analyst can theorize endlessly without clear resolution.

Sociologist Richard Sennett captured this phenomenon in his studies of craftspeople. A master carpenter doesn't need external validation to know when a joint is perfectly fitted. The knowledge lives in the hands, the eyes, the intimate understanding of materials. This kind of embodied knowledge creates what Sennett calls "quiet self-respect"— satisfaction independent of status or recognition.

Consider Kathy, who works as a school custodian in rural Minnesota. In a community profile for a local newspaper, she explained: "People think because I clean toilets for a living that I must be miserable. But I create a safe, clean space for children to learn. I know every kid by name. I notice when someone's struggling. Sometimes I'm the first adult to smile at them all day." Kathy's job is just that—a job. Her identity encompasses her role as a community elder, a gardener who supplies half the town with tomato seedlings each spring, and a woman whose kindness has shaped a generation of children.

The idea that our worth comes from our productivity is particularly crushing for those who cannot work due to disability, illness, or other circumstances. It creates a society that questions the very humanity of those who aren't economically productive. Philosopher Eva Feder Kittay, whose daughter has multiple disabilities, challenges this mindset by arguing that dependency isn't a deviation from normal human experience but an essential part of it. We are all dependent at various points in our lives—as children, when ill, as we age—and this dependency connects rather than diminishes us.

In many traditional cultures, elders who can no longer "produce" are nonetheless valued for their wisdom, their stories, their presence. Only in our hyper-individualistic, productivity-obsessed culture does reduced economic output equate to reduced human value.

Freedom from work-identity fusion doesn't mean not caring about your work. Paradoxically, when you stop defining yourself by your job, you often bring more creativity, integrity, and genuine care to what you do. Free from the desperate need for your work to validate your existence, you can approach it with curiosity rather than anxiety.

Author Annie Dillard points to this paradox in her essay "Write Till You Drop," noting that the writers who produce lasting work are rarely those most concerned with literary success. Rather, they're the ones who write because they are writers—not because writing validates them, but because it's simply what they do. The work flows from identity rather than creating it.

Look at the language we use. We don't say "I lawyer" or "I doctor." We say "I am a lawyer" or "I am a doctor." The verb "to be" fuses occupation and existence in a way other languages don't always replicate. In Spanish, one says "Soy médico" ("I am a doctor") for a permanent identity but "Estoy trabajando como médico" ("I am working as a doctor") to indicate a temporary state. The linguistic distinction preserves the separation between being and doing.

This separation isn't just philosophical—it's practical self-preservation. Industries collapse. Technologies render skills obsolete. Economies transform. If your core identity is "I am a coal miner" or "I am a newspaper journalist," economic changes don't just threaten your livelihood but your very sense of self. But if you understand yourself as a person with certain values, talents, and interests who currently mines coal or reports news, you maintain the flexibility to carry those same values into new contexts.

The path toward liberation begins with a simple question: Who would you be if you couldn't do your current work? Not what alternative job you'd choose, but who you would be as a person. What values would remain? What relationships would matter? What activities would bring meaning? The answers reveal the sturdy foundation of identity that exists beneath the superficial label of occupation.

Perhaps most importantly, separating work from identity lets us approach the inevitable question—"What should I do with my life?"—with greater ease and less desperation. When the answer doesn't have to encompass your entire being, the pressure diminishes. You're not choosing your one true calling; you're simply deciding how to spend some time, energy, and talent in exchange for the resources to live a complete life.

There's profound freedom in understanding that your job doesn't need to be your passion, your purpose, or your identity. It can simply be your job—done with integrity and care, but not burdened with the expectation that it must fulfill your every need for meaning and belonging.

Next time someone asks what you do, perhaps try answering not with your job title but with what truly animates your spirit: "I raise extraordinary children." "I build community in a fragmented world." "I create beauty where I can." "I'm working on becoming a more compassionate human." Or maybe just: "That's a complex question. Who are you beyond what pays your bills?"

The conversation that follows might be uncomfortable, unfamiliar. But in that discomfort lies the beginning of liberation—the recognition that you are vast and complex, containing multitudes far beyond what fits on a business card or LinkedIn profile. Your work is part of your life, but it isn't your life. And that revelation might be the most freeing discovery of all.

4 - The Hobby That Saves You

Something happens when no one is looking. In those unguarded moments—when the pressure to perform, to decide, to become something meaningful has temporarily lifted—we sometimes stumble upon the very thing we've been frantically searching for. It's like those dreams where you're looking everywhere for your keys, only to wake up and find them sitting plainly on the kitchen counter, where they've been all along.

The narrative we're fed about finding life's purpose runs contrary to how meaning often sneaks into our lives. We're told to search deliberately, to plan strategically, to network relentlessly. And while there's certainly value in intentionality, this essay argues for something subtler: the life-altering power of the seemingly insignificant hobby. Those activities we engage in "just because"—not to advance our careers or impress anyone—often become the unexpected saviors of our directionless periods.

Most people have experienced that peculiar suffocation that comes with the constant questioning: "What should I do with my life?" The weight of potential, the fear of wrong turns, the anxiety of watching others sprint ahead while you're still at the starting line. It's exhausting. Perhaps even more exhausting is the pressure to monetize every interest, to turn every flicker of joy into a "side hustle." But what if we've been approaching this all wrong?

There's an unassuming magic in activities pursued solely for their inherent pleasure. The garage band that never leaves the garage. The garden tended without Instagram documentation. The short stories written without submission to literary journals. These supposedly "useless" pastimes—untethered from career advancement or social capital—often become life's anchors when professional identities falter or existential questions loom too large.

Take the story of Grandma Moses, born Anna Mary Robertson. Few know that she didn't begin painting seriously until her late 70s, after arthritis made her beloved embroidery too painful. What began as a casual alternative hobby—painting rural landscapes from memory—eventually led to her work being discovered and exhibited in the Museum of Modern Art. Moses hadn't spent decades anguishing over becoming a painter; she simply found joy in the activity itself. Her hobby became her identity only in retrospect.

The path from passionate amateur to accidental professional isn't uncommon. Linux, the operating system that powers much of the internet, began as Linus Torvalds' personal hobby project—something he worked on for fun while a student at the University of Helsinki. He never intended to create something revolutionary; he simply wanted to build a system that worked the way he thought it should. In a 1991 email announcing his project, he wrote: "I'm doing a (free) operating system (just a hobby, won't be big and professional like GNU)." The humble parenthetical "just a hobby" now seems almost comical given Linux's eventual impact.

Many of us dismiss our hobbies as trivial precisely because they lack external validation. Without a paycheck or title attached, they feel somehow less legitimate. Yet paradoxically, it's often this very lack of external pressure that allows these activities to develop into something authentic and sustaining. When we remove the expectation of achievement, we create space for genuine passion to flourish.

At their best, hobbies offer a particular kind of freedom—the freedom to be terrible. A terrible painter, a terrible chess player, a terrible gardener. This permission to fail repeatedly without consequence creates psychological safety that career pursuits rarely allow. And in this safety, many find their true voice emerges. The judgment-free zone of a hobby often becomes the laboratory where we discover what actually moves us, rather than what we think should move us.

The late physicist Richard Feynman famously developed his most innovative ideas while playing with what he called "inconsequential" problems—puzzles and curiosities he explored simply because they intrigued him, not because they were part of his formal research. His work on rotating plates led to insights about quantum electrodynamics that eventually earned him a Nobel Prize. But crucially, he didn't approach these diversions with Nobel ambitions; he approached them with playfulness.

"Physics is like sex," Feynman once quipped. "Sure, it may give some practical results, but that's not why we do it." This sentiment—that the intrinsic rewards matter more than the external outcomes—lies at the heart of how hobbies subtly transform us.

In Western culture, we often maintain a strict dividing line between work and play—between the serious and the frivolous. Yet this dichotomy crumbles under scrutiny. The psychologist Mihaly Csikszentmihalyi spent decades studying "flow states"—those immersive moments when we're so absorbed in an activity that time seems to dissolve. His research revealed that people experience their most profound satisfaction not during leisure or relaxation, but during challenging activities that demand complete attention. And here's the crucial part: flow states were reported most frequently during hobbies and voluntary pursuits, not during compensated work.

Your body knows the difference between obligatory tasks and freely chosen ones, even when the activities themselves appear identical. The person who codes all day for a tech company might experience stress and burnout, while the same person coding an open-source project on weekends might find deep fulfillment. The contexts change everything.

During periods of indecision about career paths, hobbies provide something essential: they keep us moving. Motion itself has inherent value when direction feels uncertain. The bread-baking hobby that blossomed during pandemic isolation may never become a bakery business, but it taught patience, presence, and the satisfaction of creating something tangible—lessons that transcend the specific activity.

Sometimes these "useless" pursuits reveal unexpected aptitudes. The literature professor who started woodworking to relieve stress discovers she has exceptional spatial reasoning skills. The accountant who volunteers at a community theater realizes he has natural leadership abilities. These discoveries don't necessarily demand career changes, but they expand self-knowledge in ways pure introspection never could.

Too often, we try to think our way through life's big questions. We make lists of our strengths and weaknesses. We take personality assessments. We meditate on our values. While reflection has its place, there's a wisdom in the body—in the doing—that can't be accessed through contemplation alone. Hobbies engage us physically and emotionally, not just intellectually. They speak truths about ourselves that our analytical minds might miss.

Few examples illustrate this better than Julia Child, whose name became synonymous with French cooking in America. Child didn't discover her passion for cooking until she was 37 years old. Before that pivotal moment, she had worked as a copywriter and in government service during World War II. Her initial cooking classes in Paris weren't career-motivated—they were simply a way to occupy herself while her husband was stationed there for work. What began as a hobby to fill time transformed not only her life but American culinary culture itself.

In her memoir "My Life in France," Child recalls her first meal in Rouen: "It was the most exciting meal of my life." This visceral, embodied experience—not abstract career planning—set her life's direction. Sometimes we must taste something to know we hunger for it.

The contemporary obsession with productivity often leads us to devalue activities without obvious outputs or metrics. Time spent on hobbies can feel like time "wasted" in a culture that worships efficiency. But this perspective misunderstands human nature. We are not production units optimized for maximum output; we are complex beings who require varied forms of engagement to thrive.

The potter who works with clay on weekends may never sell a single piece, but the tactile connection to earth, the meditative quality of the wheel, the chemical alchemy of glazing—these experiences nourish something essential. The hobby becomes not just an activity but a relationship to material reality, a conversation between person and substance that enriches perception.

This brings us to a counterintuitive suggestion for those paralyzed by indecision about their life path: consider temporarily abandoning the question altogether. Instead of asking, "What should I do with my life?" ask, "What captures my attention regardless of its usefulness?" Follow that thread, even if it seems to lead nowhere.

The late philosopher and psychotherapist Eugene Gendlin developed a technique called "focusing," which helps people access their implicit bodily knowledge—what he called the "felt sense" of situations. Gendlin discovered that successful therapy clients naturally referred to unclear internal sensations: "there's something about this that doesn't feel right" or "I have a sense that..." Those who could attend to these subtle bodily signals, even when they couldn't immediately articulate them, made better progress than those who remained purely analytical.

Hobbies often engage this felt sense. We might not be able to explain why building model trains or learning obscure historical facts about medieval farming practices brings us satisfaction, but the body knows. The quiet enthusiasm that draws us back to an activity contains wisdom worth honoring.

A relatively unknown study from the University of Oxford tracked individuals during major life transitions—career changes, relocations, relationship shifts—and found an interesting pattern. Those who maintained consistent hobbies throughout these periods reported significantly less anxiety and greater confidence in their decisions than those without such anchors. The researchers theorized that these voluntary activities provided continuity of identity during times when professional or relational identities were in flux.

When everything else is uncertain, the weekly pottery class or chess match becomes a dependable source of self-recognition. "Even though I don't know what I'm doing with my career," the implicit thought goes, "I'm still the person who loves photographing abandoned buildings."

This thread of continuity matters more than we might realize.

The late anthropologist Mary Catherine Bateson wrote beautifully about what she called "composing a life"—the way we piece together seemingly disparate elements into a coherent whole. Rather than seeing life as a single, linear narrative, Bateson suggested we think of it as improvisational composition, where themes recur and transform. In this view, hobbies aren't mere distractions from the "real work" of building a career; they're essential threads in the tapestry.

One of the most liberating aspects of hobby-driven discovery is that it sidesteps the tyranny of talent. We live in a culture obsessed with natural aptitude, with finding that one thing we're supposedly "meant" to do. But hobbies allow us to value engagement over achievement. The joy of amateur astronomy isn't diminished by never making a novel discovery. The pleasure of recreational basketball doesn't require NBA potential.

There's a particular quality to time spent in these voluntary pursuits—a spaciousness that contracted, goal-oriented time lacks. Writer Lewis Hyde distinguishes between "work time" and what he calls "gift time." Work time is linear and exchanged for compensation. Gift time operates by different logic—it expands rather than depletes, connecting us to cycles of reciprocity and meaning that transcend market value.

Hobbies exist primarily in gift time. They remind us that not everything worthwhile can or should be monetized. In a world increasingly governed by market metrics, protecting these spaces of non-instrumental activity becomes almost countercultural.

The late poet and philosopher John O'Donohue wrote about what he called "the invisible world"—the realm of intangible but essential human experiences like love, meaning, and beauty that can't be measured but profoundly shape our lives. Hobbies often serve as doorways to this invisible world. The birdwatcher witnessing a rare migration at dawn, the amateur musician finding that perfect harmonic resolution—these moments of transcendence require no external validation.

Perhaps most importantly, hobbies can rescue us from the paralysis of perfectionism. When we remove the pressure of professional standards, we grant ourselves permission to embrace what Zen practitioners call "beginner's mind"—an attitude of openness and lack of preconceptions. This state allows for the kind of playful experimentation that often leads to genuine innovation.

Take the story of Spencer Silver, a scientist at 3M who was trying to develop a super-strong adhesive. Instead, he accidentally created an unusually weak one—a seemingly failed experiment. For years, this "mistake" had no obvious application until another 3M employee, Arthur Fry, became frustrated with paper bookmarks falling out of his hymnal during choir practice. The connection between these two unrelated problems resulted in the Post-it Note, one of the most successful office products ever created. The lesson? Innovation often happens in the spaces between formal pursuits, in the connections we make during "unproductive" time.

The British psychoanalyst D.W. Winnicott developed the concept of "transitional space"—neither fully internal nor fully external reality, but a creative in-between where play becomes possible. For adults navigating uncertainty, hobbies can provide this essential transitional space where identity can be explored without the finality of commitment.

Think of the corporate lawyer who spends weekends volunteering at an animal shelter. This activity might never become a career, but it nurtures qualities of compassion and connection that make her a more complete person—qualities that might eventually inform her legal work in unexpected ways. The boundaries between hobby and vocation aren't always clear; they often cross-pollinate in surprising fashion.

If you find yourself stuck in indecision about your life's direction, consider this approach: instead of frantically searching for your calling, create more space for purposeless joy. Pay attention to what absorbs you so completely that you lose track of time. Notice which activities you describe with excitement to friends, which topics send you down internet research rabbit holes at 2 a.m.

The path often reveals itself through accumulation of these small clues rather than through dramatic epiphany. And sometimes, the hobby itself becomes the path. The programming enthusiast who contributes to open-source projects might build relationships that lead to job opportunities. The weekend painter might eventually sell work at local art fairs. But crucially, these developments emerge organically, without strategic planning.

This isn't meant to romanticize turning passions into professions. For many, hobbies remain most valuable precisely because they stand apart from market pressures. The community theater actor who works as an electrician by day might find that keeping these worlds separate preserves the joy in both. What matters is recognizing that the supposed "side" activities often provide essential nourishment that the so-called "main" activities cannot.

For those troubled by indecision, the question becomes less "What should I do with my life?" and more "What already gives my life texture and meaning, regardless of its practical application?" The answer might be hiding in plain sight—in the garden you tend, the instruments you play, the stories you write, the games you enjoy, the problems you solve for fun.

These seemingly insignificant pursuits quietly shape us. They teach patience or spontaneity, precision or expression, solitude or collaboration. They reveal our natural rhythms and values. They speak truths about ourselves that résumés and job titles never could.

The next time indecision leaves you feeling stuck, try this radical approach: instead of forcing clarity about your future, invest more fully in those activities you already love without expectation of return. The hobby that captivates you today might just become the compass that guides you tomorrow—not because it transforms into a career, but because it reveals something essential about who you are and what kind of life feels worth living.

In the end, perhaps the most valuable thing a hobby offers isn't a potential career path but perspective—the humbling reminder that joy often arises from the spaces between our grand ambitions, in the quiet moments of doing something simply because it calls to us. And in a world obsessed with purpose and productivity, honoring that call might be the most revolutionary act of all.

5- Volunteer Like You Mean It

You're stuck. Again. Staring at the ceiling, scrolling through job listings, wondering why none of them feel right. Maybe you've made pro-con lists until your hand cramped. Maybe you've taken personality tests that tell you to become an artisanal cheese maker or a corporate lawyer—neither of which feels like you. Maybe you've journaled until the pages blurred together, an endless monologue about your potential, your passions, your purpose.

Here's a radical thought: stop thinking about yourself so much.

This flies in the face of every self-help manual ever written. The dominant wisdom says to look inward—meditate more, journal more, retreat to mountaintops or silent cabins to "find yourself." But what if the real answer isn't hidden in your psyche but outside yourself entirely? What if the solution to not knowing what to do with your life is to temporarily stop making it about your life at all?

I'm talking about volunteering, but not the kind where you show up for an hour, feel good about yourself, and leave. I'm talking about the kind that transforms you precisely because transformation isn't the goal.

When everything feels uncertain, the natural impulse is to turn inward—to analyze, reflect, and search for clarity within. We become archaeologists of our own minds, digging for clues about what we're "meant" to do. We treat our purpose like buried treasure, if only we could excavate deeply enough. But perpetual self-analysis often leads to a peculiar kind of paralysis. The more we think about what we want, the less clear it becomes. The more we obsess over finding the perfect path, the more all paths start to look equally risky or equally bland.

Action cuts through this mental fog in ways contemplation never can. Specifically, action that isn't about you—your career anxiety, your existential dread, your quarter-life or midlife crisis. Volunteer work creates what psychologists call a "focusing illusion reset." When you're genuinely absorbed in helping others, the questions that haunt you— What am I passionate about? What should I do with my life?—temporarily dissolve. Not because they're answered, but because they're replaced by more immediate concerns: This person needs food. This beach needs cleaning. This child needs to learn to read.

The counterintuitive beauty here is that by stepping away from your existential questions, you often stumble upon answers. Not tidy, fortune-cookie answers, but lived insights that couldn't have emerged any other way.

The neuroscience backs this up. When we help others, our brains release oxytocin, serotonin, and dopamine—the trifecta of feel-good neurochemicals. These don't just make us feel warm and fuzzy; they literally change how we think. Researchers at Emory University found that altruism activates the same reward centers in our brains as food and sex. But unlike those fleeting pleasures, the neurological benefits of helping others can last for hours or even days.

This isn't just about feeling better, though that's certainly a bonus when you're mired in indecision and doubt. It's about creating new neural pathways—literally changing your brain's architecture through experience rather than through thought exercises or affirmations. You're building what neuroplasticity researchers call "experience-dependent plasticity," reshaping your brain not through thinking about what you want, but through doing what is needed.

There's something else happening, too, something subtler but perhaps more profound. When you volunteer, especially in sustained ways, you temporarily step outside the market economy. You're no longer a consumer or a producer or a commodity. You're not being paid; your value isn't being measured in dollars or promotions. This creates a rare kind of freedom—freedom from the pressure to monetize your time, to optimize your skills, to constantly assess your market value.

In the absence of these pressures, different questions emerge. Not "What should I do with my life?" but "What needs doing right now?" Not "What am I passionate about?" but "What problems am I willing to help solve, even when it's tedious or difficult?" Not "What will make me happy?" but "What contribution matters, regardless of how it makes me feel?"

These questions don't replace the search for meaningful work. They reframe it. They ground abstract existential quandaries in concrete human needs. They turn your focus outward, toward the world that needs changing, rather than inward, toward the self that needs fulfilling.

After the 2011 Fukushima disaster in Japan, something remarkable happened. Thousands of retired professionals—engineers, doctors, teachers—came out of retirement to volunteer in the recovery efforts. They became known as the "gray army," and their contribution was immeasurable. But what's most interesting isn't what they gave; it's what they reported receiving: a renewed sense of purpose, unexpected joy, and for many, a complete recalibration of what they thought "mattered" in life.

One retired accountant, Hiroshi Yamada, had spent decades meticulously tracking numbers for a large corporation. After volunteering to help displaced families navigate the bureaucratic maze of government assistance, he told a reporter: "I spent forty years thinking my talent was working with numbers. Now I realize my talent is patience with people who are frustrated. I wish I had known this earlier, but I am grateful to know it now."

Yamada's story illustrates what researchers call "self-knowledge through social interaction"—the idea that we discover who we are not through introspection alone, but through engagement with others and the world. This isn't mystical; it's deeply practical. You can't know how you'll respond to a crisis until you're in one. You can't know what kinds of problems energize rather than drain you until you've faced different kinds of problems. You can't know what impact you're capable of having until you've tried to have an impact.

The volunteer experience also offers something else: a chance to try on different roles without the pressure of commitment. Think of it as career speed-dating. You might discover that you love teaching but hate administrative work. You might find that you thrive in crisis situations but struggle with long-term projects. You might realize you have a gift for explaining complex ideas to people without technical backgrounds. These insights don't come from personality tests or career counselors; they come from real-world experience.

And sometimes, yes, volunteering leads directly to new career paths. A 2018 LinkedIn survey found that 41% of hiring managers consider volunteer work equally as valuable as paid work experience when evaluating candidates. More importantly, 20% of hiring managers said they had personally hired someone because of their volunteer experience. Not because volunteering checked a corporate social responsibility box, but because it demonstrated skills, adaptability, and character.

But focusing too much on these practical benefits misses the deeper point. The greatest value of volunteering when you're lost isn't that it might lead to a job. It's that it reconnects you with the fundamental truth that your work —paid or unpaid—exists in relationship to others. It exists to solve problems, meet needs, create value. In a culture obsessed with self-fulfillment and personal branding, this perspective is revolutionary.

The question shifts from "What should I do with my life?" to "What does life ask of me?" The German philosopher

Martin Buber captured this when he wrote about the difference between "I-It" relationships, where others are objects to be used, and "I-Thou" relationships, where we encounter others in their full humanity. In I-Thou relationships, we don't just act upon the world; we respond to it. We enter into dialogue with reality rather than imposing our will upon it.

This responsiveness—this willingness to let the world's needs shape our contribution rather than insisting that our contribution fit some preconceived notion of our identity—lies at the heart of meaningful work. Not just volunteer work, but all work worthy of our humanity.

Of course, there's a shadow side to volunteering that we must acknowledge. The "voluntourism" industry—short-term, often expensive volunteer trips to developing countries—has been rightly criticized for prioritizing wealthy Westerners' desire for transformative experiences over the actual needs of communities. There's a thin line between genuine service and using others' hardship as a backdrop for your personal growth journey.

But this criticism points to an important truth: the best volunteering isn't about you finding yourself. It's about you forgetting yourself enough to be genuinely useful. The personal transformation happens not because you sought it, but because you sought something else entirely: to meet a need, to solve a problem, to ease suffering, to create beauty, to protect what's valuable.

Jack Kornfield, the Buddhist teacher, tells a story about a man who spent years searching for the perfect teacher and the perfect spiritual practice. After traveling the world and studying with masters of various traditions, he finally found a teacher who seemed truly enlightened. "What is your practice?" the seeker asked. "I chop wood and carry water for the monastery," the teacher replied. The seeker, thinking he had misunderstood, asked again. The teacher smiled and said, "When I'm hungry, I eat. When I'm tired, I sleep. And during the day, I chop wood and carry water, because that's what the community needs."

The story illuminates something essential: meaning often emerges not from grand callings or perfect alignment between your passions and your work, but from meeting the needs in front of you with full presence and care. There is profound dignity in doing what needs to be done, not because it fulfills your unique purpose, but because it needs doing and you are there to do it.

This doesn't mean abandoning your search for work that engages your specific talents and interests. It means approaching that search with less anxiety and more openness. It means recognizing that purpose isn't just found; it's built, relationship by relationship, task by task, contribution by contribution.

When I talk with people who feel stuck in their careers or uncertain about their direction, I often suggest a simple but challenging exercise: commit to a volunteer role that stretches you in some way, that puts you in contact with people or problems outside your usual orbit. Not for a day or a week, but for at least three months. Enough time to move beyond the initial excitement or discomfort, to experience the full reality of the work.

The only rule is that you have to choose something that isn't obviously connected to your current career or the career you think you want. If you're in finance, don't volunteer to help a nonprofit with their accounting. If you're considering becoming a teacher, don't volunteer at a school. The goal isn't to test-drive a specific career; it's to step completely outside your current frame of reference.

What happens next varies widely. Some people discover unexpected passions or talents that do lead to career changes. A lawyer who volunteers at a community garden might discover a love for landscape design. A marketing executive who volunteers with hospice patients might feel drawn to nursing or counseling.

But more often, the transformation is subtler. People don't necessarily change what they do; they change how they think about what they do. They bring the perspective gained through volunteering back to their existing work. They find ways to incorporate more direct service into their current roles. They become more intentional about how their skills can address real needs, whether that's through their paid work or alongside it.

And some discover that what they've been seeking through career changes might actually be available through committed volunteer work alongside a job that simply pays the bills without great existential weight. Not everyone needs to find their ultimate purpose through their paycheck.

The writer and civil rights activist Howard Thurman said, "Don't ask what the world needs. Ask what makes you come alive, and go do it. Because what the world needs is people who have come alive." This quote is often used to justify pursuing your passion above all else. But I think Thurman was pointing to something deeper: that genuine aliveness comes not from self-fulfillment but from meaningful engagement with the world and others.

Sometimes we come alive precisely when we stop obsessing over what makes us come alive and instead respond to what's in front of us with presence and care. The question isn't whether to follow your passion or meet the world's needs; it's how to find the fertile ground where your aliveness and the world's needs intersect.

So if you're stuck—if you're paralyzed by indecision about what to do with your life—volunteer like you mean it. Not as a line on your resume, not as a way to network, not even primarily as a way to find your purpose. Volunteer because the world is full of problems that need solving, people who need caring for, beauty that needs creating and protecting. Volunteer because action trumps analysis when you're stuck in your head. Volunteer because sometimes the most important growth happens when you stop trying to grow and simply try to be useful.

You might not find the perfect answer to what you should do with your life. But you might find something better: the recognition that your life was never just about you to begin with. And in that recognition lies a paradoxical freedom— freedom from the endless pressure to optimize your existence, to maximize your potential, to find the perfect fit.

Purpose isn't a prize hidden at the end of a perfect decision-making process. It's a relationship between your unique gifts and the world's real needs. And relationships aren't figured out in advance; they're built day by day, choice by choice, action by action.

So put down the personality test, close the journal, postpone the meditation retreat. Find something that needs doing—something concrete, something that matters to people other than yourself—and do it wholeheartedly for a while. Not forever, just long enough to get outside your own head and remember that you exist in a world that needs you, not for some grand purpose you haven't discovered yet, but for the thousand small purposes that are visible everywhere when you start looking outward instead of inward.

Your life's work will find you when you stop tending so carefully to your uncertainty and start tending, even imperfectly, to the world.

6 - The Beauty of Being Decent at a Lot of Things

You've heard it a thousand times—the breathless advice to "find your passion" and "specialize early." From elementary school through adulthood, we're nudged toward becoming specialists, masters of singular domains. The narrative is seductive: pick one thing, pour your heart into it, become exceptional. Meanwhile, those who dabble in multiple interests are labeled "jack of all trades, master of none," a phrase that somehow always sounds dismissive, even accusatory.

But what if we've been telling ourselves the wrong story?

There's an unsung glory in being reasonably good at many things—a hidden power in breadth that our culture of hyper-specialization often misses. The world doesn't just need specialists; it needs connectors, translators, people who can weave disparate threads into something new. And sometimes, those people are the ones who never quite settled on a single passion.

When I talk to friends struggling with career indecision, they often frame it as failure—as if their inability to commit to one path is a character flaw rather than a different kind of strength. They feel inadequate next to colleagues who knew they wanted to be neurosurgeons since age twelve or friends who've been coding since middle school. Yet many of these same "indecisive" friends are the ones I call when I need creative solutions to complex problems. Their minds move differently, seeing patterns and possibilities that specialists miss.

Growing up in a small town, I knew a man named Carl who fixed machinery, played three instruments in weekend bands, wrote surprisingly good poetry, and maintained the most beautiful vegetable garden in the county. He wasn't world-class at any single one of these pursuits, but the combination made him irreplaceable in our community. When the local school needed someone to repair their ancient boiler *and* teach the kids basic music theory after their teacher left mid-year, guess who stepped in? Carl wasn't just surviving with his diverse skills—he was thriving precisely because of them.

David Epstein explores this phenomenon beautifully in his book *Range*, where he challenges the notion that early specialization is the only path to success. Through research spanning sports, science, and the arts, Epstein demonstrates how generalists often outperform specialists, particularly in complex, unpredictable environments. He tells the story of Roger Federer, who played a wide variety of sports as a child before focusing on tennis—contrary to the Tiger Woods model of hyperfocused specialization from toddlerhood. Federer's diverse athletic background may have contributed to his creative, adaptable playing style and extraordinary career longevity.

The value of breadth isn't just anecdotal. Modern workplaces increasingly reward those who can synthesize information across domains. The designer who understands both aesthetics and user psychology. The doctor with enough business acumen to improve healthcare systems. The programmer who can also write clear, compelling documentation. These hybrid skills don't emerge from narrow focus but from curious exploration across boundaries.

Behind the scenes of almost every major innovation, you'll find people working at the intersection of fields. Take Lonni Sue Johnson, an illustrator whose work appeared on the covers of The New Yorker and in publications for NASA, Princeton, and The New York Times. Johnson was also an accomplished amateur pilot and classical musician. When viral encephalitis destroyed her ability to form new memories, researchers studying her case discovered something remarkable: her cognitive flexibility allowed her to develop new artistic techniques despite profound amnesia. The connections between her varied interests had created neural pathways that proved surprisingly resilient.

Maybe you've felt embarrassed about your diverse resume or the way your interests refuse to follow a straight line. Perhaps you've watched peers climb specialized career ladders while you moved sideways, exploring new territories. There's an undercurrent of anxiety when people ask, "So what do you do?" and you don't have a neat, one-word answer. But that complexity might be your greatest asset.

The investor Charlie Munger, Warren Buffett's long-time business partner, speaks often about his "latticework of mental models"—the idea that wisdom comes from understanding fundamental concepts across disciplines. Physics, psychology, mathematics, biology, history—all provide frameworks for understanding the world. "To the man with only a hammer," Munger says, "every problem looks like a nail." But to the person with many tools, the world reveals its true complexity.

We live in an age that worships expertise, and for good reason. Specialization has given us medical breakthroughs, technological revolutions, and profound artistic achievements. The deep focus of experts provides value that breadth alone cannot match. But alongside this crucial depth, we need the bridges that generalists build between specialized islands of knowledge.

This isn't about abandoning mastery—it's about redefining it. True mastery might not be about reaching the absolute pinnacle of one narrow field, but about developing sufficient skill in multiple areas and finding the unique power in their combination.

Consider the emergence of entirely new fields born from the intersection of traditional disciplines: bioengineering, behavioral economics, computational linguistics. These hybrid domains often attract those who never quite fit the conventional academic molds, those comfortable living between established territories.

Anna Kerrigan, a relatively unknown name outside specialized circles, exemplifies this power of intersection. After studying both neuroscience and theater design—an unusual combination by any standard—she pioneered therapeutic environments for children with sensory processing disorders. The science informed the design; the design brought the science to life. Neither discipline alone would have produced her innovations. When interviewed about her unconventional career path, Kerrigan admitted she once felt "hopelessly unfocused" compared to her more specialized peers. Now she recognizes that her winding path wasn't a failure to commit but a necessary journey to her unique contribution.

The permission to be decent at many things rather than exceptional at one thing can be profoundly liberating. It allows for a kind of intellectual play that specialization sometimes squeezes out. When you're not investing your entire identity in being "the best" at something, you can approach learning with genuine curiosity rather than competitive anxiety. You can take risks, make mistakes, and follow tangents that might lead nowhere—or might lead everywhere.

This isn't just philosophical—it's practical. The modern economy is characterized by rapid change and disruption. The hyperspecialized can find themselves vulnerable when their particular expertise becomes automated or obsolete. Meanwhile, those with diverse skills can adapt, combining their capabilities in new ways as circumstances change. The software engineer who also understands design principles and client communication doesn't just become a better engineer—they become recession-proof in ways their more narrowly focused colleagues might not.

I'm reminded of a violinist friend who spent decades mastering her instrument, only to develop tendonitis that ended her professional performance career. In her darkest moment, she realized that music had consumed so much of her identity that she hardly knew who she was without it. Her recovery—both physical and psychological—came partly through exploring interests she'd previously set aside: teaching, composition, and even instrument repair. She'd always been decent at these things but had focused exclusively on performance. Now, years later, she runs a thriving music education business that draws on all these skills. "I'm not the world's greatest teacher or luthier," she told me, "but I'm good enough at several things that together make something special."

This isn't to diminish the value of dedication or deep expertise. There's something magnificent about those who devote themselves completely to mastering one domain. We need heart surgeons who've performed thousands of operations, not hundreds. We need research scientists who've spent decades understanding specific biological mechanisms. But we also need those who move between worlds, translating specialized knowledge into forms more widely accessible and applicable.

The generalist's path requires its own kind of courage. It means resisting the pressure to define yourself narrowly. It means accepting that you might never experience the particular satisfaction of being indisputably "the best" at something. Instead, you'll find different pleasures: making connections others miss, adapting quickly when circumstances change, bringing fresh perspectives to established fields.

This courage is what I saw in Marcus, a young man I met while researching this essay. Marcus studied engineering in college but also took classes in psychology, design, and business. After graduation, he joined an engineering firm but quickly became restless. Rather than forcing himself to focus exclusively on engineering, he began volunteering with a nonprofit developing affordable housing solutions. There, his engineering knowledge combined with his broader understanding of human needs and financial constraints allowed him to suggest practical improvements that more specialized team members had overlooked. Today, Marcus works at the intersection of technology and social impact, a position that wouldn't exist for someone with a more conventional career path.

"I used to think I was doing something wrong," Marcus told me. "Everyone else seemed so certain about their career tracks. But now I realize my meandering path wasn't aimless—it was exploratory. I wasn't failing to specialize; I was preparing for work that doesn't fit neatly into existing categories."

The beauty of being decent at many things isn't just professional—it enriches personal life as well. The ability to cook a satisfying meal, fix basic household problems, play an instrument well enough for personal enjoyment, speak a second language conversationally, write clearly about topics that matter to you—these skills don't need to reach professional levels to add texture and autonomy to daily life.

There's also something deeply human about this approach to learning and growth. Before the modern age of hyperspecialization, most people needed varied competencies simply to survive. A farmer didn't just grow crops; they constructed buildings, repaired tools, preserved food, and negotiated trades. An artisan wasn't just a craftsperson but often a merchant, teacher, and community leader as well. Our specialized society has brought tremendous benefits, but perhaps at the cost of that fundamental human experience of versatility.

The generalist's approach aligns with what psychologists call a "growth mindset"—the belief that abilities can be developed through dedication and hard work. When you're not defining success as reaching the absolute pinnacle of one field, you're free to embrace learning across many domains without fear of "not being good enough." This mindset creates resilience. Setbacks in one area don't devastate your entire sense of self because your identity isn't bound to singular mastery.

And what of that old saying, "jack of all trades, master of none"? Few people know the complete phrase: "Jack of all trades, master of none, though oftentimes better than master of one." The original meaning wasn't derogatory but acknowledged the special value of versatility.

As you navigate the question of what to do with your life, consider embracing the beauty of being decent at many things. Not as a consolation prize for failing to find your "one true calling," but as a deliberate choice with its own rewards. Perhaps true fulfillment doesn't come from climbing to the top of a single mountain but from exploring the varied landscape of your own curiosity, building connections between different kinds of knowledge, and creating value in the spaces between established domains.

The world needs its specialists, its virtuosos focused on pushing particular boundaries. But it equally needs its renaissance people, its polymaths, its generalists—those comfortable dwelling in multiple worlds and speaking multiple languages, literal or figurative. Both paths have dignity. Both create value. And in a world growing ever more complex and interconnected, the ability to weave between specialized domains might be not just valuable but essential.

So the next time someone asks what you do—and your answer doesn't fit neatly into a single category—stand a little taller. Your diverse interests and abilities aren't a failure to find your path. They are your path, unique and valuable precisely because of their multiplicity. In the ecology of human capability, you're not a monoculture but a diverse forest, offering many kinds of fruit, shelter, and beauty. And in that diversity lies a resilience and creative potential that no single specialization, however impressive, can match.

7 - What Sports Can Teach You About Losing with Purpose

The scoreboard flashes its final numbers. The crowd falls silent, or worse, begins to disperse early—leaving only the hollow echo of your own breathing in the arena. You've lost. Again. And not just any loss, but the kind that matters: the championship game, the promotion-deciding match, the Olympic final you've spent four years visualizing. There's a peculiar alchemy to these moments—the way defeat transmutes something solid inside you into something hollow. The way your body suddenly feels both leaden and insubstantial.

But what if I told you that this feeling—this empty, aching moment—might be the most valuable gift sports has to offer?

Not the victories. Not the highlight reels. The losses.

The world loves winners. Society venerates them, studies them, asks them to write memoirs and give commencement speeches. But in our obsession with winning, we've created a dangerous narrative around losing: that it's merely a stepping stone on the path to eventual victory, a necessary evil, something to be overcome rather than understood. Yet the most profound lessons from sports come not from those who consistently triumph, but from those who lose with purpose—those who understand that defeat isn't just an unfortunate outcome but a powerful teacher in its own right.

Our lives mirror athletic competition in more ways than we admit. We compete for jobs, recognition, love, attention. We track metrics, compare ourselves to peers, and live with the constant undercurrent of performance anxiety. Many of us operate within internal scorecards far more punishing than any Olympic judge's tablet. And yet, unlike athletes who train explicitly for the psychology of winning and losing, most of us remain woefully unprepared for life's inevitable defeats.

In the summer of 1992, a British athlete named Derek Redmond lined up for the semifinal of the 400-meter race at the Barcelona Olympics. He was a favorite to medal, having set the British record and won gold at the World Championships. But 150 meters into the race, his hamstring tore with a pop so loud that cameras picked up the sound. What happened next has become one of the most famous Olympic moments in history—not because of athletic excellence, but because of athletic heartbreak. Redmond, collapsed in agony, refused to quit. He rose and began hopping toward the finish line on one leg. His father broke through security and helped him complete the race, with Redmond sobbing on his shoulder.

What makes this moment so profound wasn't just the pain or determination, but the transformation happening inside Redmond's mind. In interviews years later, he revealed that crossing that finish line—last place, disqualified— became more significant to him than any medal could have been. "I went to those Olympics to win gold," he said. "I never did. But I went home with something better."

The story sounds like a Hollywood script, and indeed, it became the stuff of Nike commercials and motivational posters. But the less discussed truth is what happened in the years after. Redmond never regained his previous form. He attempted comebacks but eventually retired from track and field. The conventional wisdom would call this a tragedy—the athlete who never achieved his potential. But Redmond later found success as a basketball player, then as a motorcycle racer, and eventually as a motivational speaker. His life became defined not by Olympic gold but by his response to its absence.

Too often, we approach life decisions as if they're Olympic finals. We expect our careers, relationships, and personal ambitions to follow the arc of a sports movie: struggle, breakthrough, triumph. We've been taught that failure is only meaningful if it eventually leads to success in the same arena. But what if the true meaning of failure is in how it reveals the other arenas where we might thrive? What if losing with purpose isn't about getting back up to try the same thing again, but about discovering what else we might be meant to do?

The Finnish have a concept called "sisu," which roughly translates to determination and stoic perseverance. But it's not just about grit or resilience. Sisu is about finding reserves of strength during moments of extreme adversity —not to conquer the adversity, but to transform alongside it. It acknowledges that sometimes, the goal isn't to overcome the obstacle but to be changed by it.

In 1986, a small football club in northern England called Middlesbrough FC was hours away from liquidation. The club, beloved in its community for over a century, had run out of money and was about to cease existing. No dramatic rescue from wealthy investors appeared. Instead, a group of local supporters, led by a 29-year-old employee named Steve Gibson, scraped together enough money to save the club—not to make it successful, but just to keep it alive. The team was relegated to a lower division and played in a nearly empty stadium. For years, they were, by conventional metrics, losers.

Yet something remarkable happened during those wilderness years. The relationship between the club and its remaining supporters deepened. Without the pressure of competing at the highest level, the team became more embedded in its community. They started youth programs, opened their training grounds to local schools, and players began visiting hospitals and community centers. When success eventually returned years later (the club would reach a European final in 2006), the foundation built during those losing years proved more valuable than any trophy.

This pattern repeats across sports history. The teams and athletes we remember most fondly aren't always the ones with the most championships. They're the ones who lose with character and purpose—who transform defeat into something more meaningful than victory could have been.

When considering your own life path and the paralyzing indecision that comes with it, perhaps the first question isn't "What am I meant to succeed at?" but rather, "What am I willing to lose at?" What endeavor matters enough that you would endure repeated failure for its sake? What pursuit would still feel meaningful even if traditional success never materialized?

Tom Brady, arguably the greatest quarterback in NFL history, speaks often about Super Bowl XLII—the championship game that cost his New England Patriots team a perfect season. "I remember after the game I was crying, thinking about that game," Brady said years later. "I still remember the feeling in my stomach when we lost." But what's remarkable about Brady isn't just his six championship rings; it's how he metabolized that crushing defeat. He didn't just use it as motivation to win more; he fundamentally changed his approach to the game, his training regimen, and even his personal life in ways that reflected the lessons of that loss.

The true masters of any craft aren't those who win most often; they're those who extract the most wisdom from their losses. They don't just endure defeat—they examine it, inhabit it, and ultimately transform it.

For those of us struggling with life direction, this perspective offers an alternative to the paralysis of endless options. Instead of asking which path guarantees success, we might consider which paths contain failures we're willing to accept—even embrace—as part of our journey.

Swiss psychiatrist Elisabeth Kübler-Ross famously developed the five stages of grief that help us understand how people process loss. But her work has broader implications when applied to the smaller deaths we experience in daily life: the death of a dream, an expectation, a cherished self-image. Athletes at the highest level intuitively understand these stages—denial, anger, bargaining, depression, acceptance—because they cycle through them with every significant defeat.

The 1994 Winter Olympics in Lillehammer gave us an unforgettable example of this cycle in real-time. Dan Jansen, America's premier speed skater, had become known as much for his Olympic heartbreak as for his world records. In the 1988 Games, he had fallen in both his races after learning of his sister's death from leukemia hours before competing. In 1992, he failed again to medal. By 1994, at age 28, Lillehammer represented his final Olympic opportunity. When he fell in his strongest event, the 500 meters, the narrative seemed tragically sealed. But four days later, in the 1000 meters—an event in which he wasn't favored—Jansen skated the race of his life and won gold.

What made this moment transcendent wasn't just the comeback narrative. It was the visible transformation of a man who had fully metabolized his losses. In interviews after his victory, Jansen spoke not about redemption but about liberation. "I didn't need the gold medal to justify my career or my life," he said. "Somewhere along the way, I figured out that there are more important things than winning or losing races."

This sentiment—that the medal wasn't the point—wasn't empty rhetoric. It was the hard-won wisdom of someone who had learned to lose with purpose. Jansen didn't overcome his failures; he integrated them into a more expansive understanding of his life's meaning.

For those of us facing indecision about careers, relationships, or life direction, this offers a profound reframing. The question isn't whether we'll experience failure—we will. The question is whether those failures will feel purposeful, whether they'll connect to something larger than our individual achievement.

A less well-known but equally instructive case comes from the 2004 Athens Olympics. Australian swimmer Leisel Jones, then just 18, entered as the world record holder and overwhelming favorite in the 100-meter breaststroke. She left with a bronze medal, openly weeping on the podium in what commentators described as one of the Olympics' most visible displays of disappointment. For Jones, who had spent her young life pursuing Olympic gold with single-minded focus, the moment represented more than athletic disappointment—it was an identity crisis.

What happened next defied the conventional narrative. Rather than redoubling her training or making drastic changes to her technique, Jones did something far more radical: she prioritized her happiness over her ambition. She began working with a sports psychologist not to enhance performance but to reconnect with the joy that had initially drawn her to swimming. She loosened her rigid training schedule and allowed herself to enjoy life outside the pool.

The results were counterintuitive. Four years later in Beijing, a more relaxed Jones won the gold medal that had eluded her, swimming faster than she had in Athens. But in interviews afterward, she was clear: "Winning wasn't what made me happy. Finding joy in the process again—that's what mattered."

Jones' story illustrates a paradox central to both sports and life: sometimes we need to care less about the outcome to achieve our best results. More importantly, her journey demonstrates how losing with purpose often means excavating the original meaning of our pursuits from beneath the accumulated weight of expectations and external validation.

Psychologists use the term "post-traumatic growth" to describe the positive psychological changes that can follow significant adversity or trauma. While athletic defeats don't compare to genuine trauma, they often trigger similar psychological mechanisms. Athletes who lose with purpose don't just recover from defeat—they expand their capacity for complexity, deepen their empathy, and discover new dimensions of meaning.

In 2016, Norwegian swimmer Alexander Dale Oen was favored to win gold in the 100-meter breaststroke at the London Olympics. During a training camp three months before the Games, he died suddenly of a heart attack at just 26 years old. His teammate and closest friend, Henrik Christiansen, was devastated. Christiansen had been training alongside Dale Oen with his own Olympic dreams. After Dale Oen's death, Christiansen considered quitting the sport altogether.

Instead, he found himself swimming with a transformed purpose. "Before, I was swimming for medals," he told reporters. "After Alexander died, I started swimming for something else—for the joy he brought to it, for the way he made people feel about themselves."

Christiansen never won an Olympic medal. By conventional metrics, his athletic career might be considered less successful than many of his peers. But the meaning he found in swimming—the way he used the sport to process grief and honor his friend's memory—transcended any podium finish.

For those of us facing indecision about our life direction, this reframing offers a valuable lens. Perhaps the question isn't "What am I meant to succeed at?" but "What would still feel meaningful even if success, as conventionally defined, never comes?"

Many of sports' most powerful lessons about losing with purpose come not from the glamorous, televised arenas of professional leagues but from its overlooked corners—community leagues, small college programs, and particularly, adaptive sports for athletes with disabilities.

The Paralympic Games represent perhaps the purest distillation of losing with purpose. Every Paralympic athlete has already experienced profound loss—of limbs, sight, mobility, or neurological function. Yet they've transformed those losses into the foundation of new identities and achievements. What's remarkable isn't just their physical resilience but their psychological alchemy—the ability to convert what might be seen as deficit into difference, and difference into advantage.

Tatyana McFadden, born with spina bifida and paralyzed from the waist down, spent her early years in a Russian orphanage before being adopted by an American family. She has since won 17 Paralympic medals across multiple sports and distances. When asked about her success, McFadden doesn't focus on overcoming her disability but on the unique strengths it helped her develop. "I don't succeed despite my disability," she once said. "In many ways, I succeed because of it. It shaped how I see challenges, how I respond to setbacks."

McFadden's perspective offers a powerful framework for anyone facing indecision or feeling lost. Perhaps our greatest strengths aren't despite our struggles but because of them. Perhaps the very things we've lost—opportunities, relationships, certain paths not taken—are precisely what equip us for the paths we're meant to find.

In his book "The Obstacle Is the Way," Ryan Holiday examines how ancient Stoic philosophers viewed adversity not as something to be avoided but as the essential material from which a meaningful life is constructed. "The impediment to action advances action," wrote Marcus Aurelius. "What stands in the way becomes the way."

Few athletic careers better illustrate this principle than that of Wilma Rudolph. Born prematurely in 1940 in segregated Tennessee, Rudolph contracted infantile paralysis (caused by polio) at age four. She wore a leg brace until she was nine and was told she would never walk normally. Yet she not only walked—she ran. At the 1960 Rome Olympics, she became the first American woman to win three gold medals in a single Games, earning the title "the fastest woman in the world."

What's less known about Rudolph is what happened after her athletic career ended. She became a teacher and coach in impoverished communities, focusing particularly on helping young girls who, like her, faced seemingly insurmountable obstacles. When asked about this choice, Rudolph was clear: "My greatest accomplishment was not winning those medals but coming back to Tennessee and working with young people."

For Rudolph, athletic success wasn't the destination but the vehicle—a means of developing the wisdom and platform she would use for her deeper purpose. Her story suggests that perhaps our periods of indecision and uncertainty aren't detours from our proper path but essential preparation for it.

This brings us to perhaps the most profound lesson sports teaches about losing with purpose: the idea that meaning isn't found in isolated moments of triumph but in the continuity of effort across time. The Roman philosopher Seneca wrote that "life is long if you know how to use it." Athletes who lose with purpose understand this intuitively. They know that no single victory or defeat defines them.

What matters is the ongoing commitment to growth and meaning-making.

In 2008, swimmer Dara Torres qualified for the US Olympic team at age 41—her fifth Olympic Games across three decades. She had stepped away from the sport twice, once to start a family and once simply because she'd lost passion for competition. Yet each time she returned, it wasn't to recapture former glory but to discover new aspects of herself through the familiar discipline of swimming.

In Beijing, Torres won three silver medals, finishing just one-hundredth of a second behind the gold medalist in the 50-meter freestyle. That microscopic margin might have devastated a younger athlete, but Torres beamed on the podium. "I've already won," she told reporters. "The race is just a moment. The journey is the achievement."

Torres embodied what psychologists call a "mastery orientation" rather than a "performance orientation." She measured herself not against others but against her own evolving potential. For those of us facing indecision, this shift in perspective is liberating. What if success isn't about finding the one perfect path but about bringing our fullest engagement to whichever path we choose?

The deeper wisdom here has implications beyond career choices or life direction. It speaks to how we move through the world—how we approach not just our ambitions but our relationships, our communities, our inner lives. In a culture obsessed with optimization and achievement, learning to lose with purpose is a radical act. It asserts that meaning transcends measurement, that the unmapped journey holds as much value as the destination.

Sports, at its best, teaches us this truth. Not through highlight reels or championship parades, but through those quiet moments when athletes—having given everything and still fallen short—discover something more valuable than victory. They discover themselves.

So as you stand at life's crossroads, paralyzed by the infinity of possible paths, perhaps the question isn't "Which path leads to success?" but "Which path's failures will teach me what I most need to learn?" Not "Where will I win?" but "Where will my losses feel meaningful?"

Because in the end, we're all going to lose. We'll lose games, opportunities, relationships, health, and ultimately, life itself. The question isn't whether we'll face defeat but whether we'll face it with purpose—whether we'll allow our losses to hollow us out or to create space for something new to grow.

The scoreboard will always eventually go dark. The stadium will empty. The medals will tarnish. What remains is not what we won or lost, but who we became in the attempt.

8 - Screw the Ladder – Build a Web

The career ladder is an image that haunts us. It's there in glossy company brochures, in the PowerPoint slides of corporate orientations, in the dreams our parents had for us. The ladder is simple: climb it, make more money, get a better title, gain more power, and somehow, magically, arrive at a place of career fulfillment. It's clean. It's orderly. It's brutal.

What if I told you the ladder was a lie? Not just a small fib —a comprehensive, damaging fabrication that has done more to trap people in careers they hate than almost any other concept. The ladder is a myth that doesn't match how work actually unfolds in the 21st century, or how humans naturally develop.

No one told Marie this. At thirty-seven, she had been climbing the ladder at her finance firm for fifteen years. Associate to manager to director to senior director—each rung bringing marginally more pay and substantially more stress. When I met her, she was sitting in her corner office, surrounded by the evidence of her "success," telling me how empty she felt.

"I did everything they said I should," she explained, her voice hollow. "I put in the eighty-hour weeks. I skipped vacations. I networked with the right people. I have the title and the salary my twenty-year-old self would have killed for. And I hate Monday mornings with every fiber of my being."

Marie had fallen for the ladder myth. She believed that vertical ascension was the only path worth pursuing. That each rung would bring her closer to some elusive sense of arrival. But here's what nobody ever mentions about ladders: they only go in one direction. They force you into a narrow channel of development. And when you finally reach the top—if there even is a "top"—there's often nothing there except thin air and the acute realization that you've been climbing the wrong structure altogether.

This isn't just Marie's problem. It's embedded in our language around work. We "climb the corporate ladder." We "work our way up." We celebrate the "rise" to the top. All of these metaphors reinforce the same broken idea: that career development is singular, linear, and vertical.

But what if there's another way? What if, instead of a ladder, we envision a web?

A web has multiple anchoring points. It expands outward, not just upward. It creates connections between seemingly unrelated parts. It's adaptive, organic, and far more resilient than a ladder could ever be. If one strand breaks, the rest of the web holds.

The web model reflects how careers actually work now. Anthropologist Gillian Tett's research into how people actually navigate modern careers revealed something fascinating: those who thrived most weren't just climbing upward—they were moving laterally, diagonally, sometimes even backward, accumulating skills and experiences that wouldn't fit on a traditional resume. They were creating webs of competence and connection, not just climbing ladders.

Take Stefan, a man I met while researching this book. He started as a software developer at a major tech company. Instead of simply gunning for the next promotion, he volunteered for projects that interested him, regardless of whether they were considered "prestigious." He learned marketing basics while helping a team launch a new product. He picked up public speaking by presenting at internal conferences. He dabbled in UX design by shadowing the designers on his project.

When layoffs hit his company, Stefan wasn't devastated. His web of skills and relationships led him to a small startup where he became a product manager—a role that perfectly utilized his hybrid skill set. Later, those same diverse experiences helped him launch his own consulting business. Had Stefan focused only on climbing the traditional developer ladder, he would have been vulnerable when that single path disappeared.

The web approach isn't just more resilient—it's more aligned with what humans actually enjoy. Research in occupational psychology consistently shows that people are happiest when they can express multiple facets of their personalities and skills in their work. Few of us are truly content being one-dimensional specialists forever.

The ladder mentality forces us to shed parts of ourselves to fit the narrow role above us. The web mentality lets us integrate more of who we are into our work. It honors complexity. It celebrates the meandering path.

Perhaps nobody embodies this better than Kara Walker, whose artistic career defies categorization. Known primarily as a visual artist, Walker has refused to climb only the "become a more famous painter" ladder. Instead, she's built a web that includes installation art, shadow puppetry, film, and writing. Her work appears everywhere from museum walls to public parks. By refusing to limit herself to one medium or audience, she's created a career that's uniquely hers—and far more interesting than had she simply climbed a single ladder of success.

The web approach also corresponds with how innovation actually happens. Throughout history, breakthroughs haven't come from specialists who climb ever higher in their narrow fields. They come from people who build connections between different domains.

James Burke's landmark television series "Connections" demonstrated this beautifully. He traced how innovations rarely follow a straight path. Instead, they emerge from unexpected intersections of ideas and technologies. The development of the computer, for instance, was influenced by the punch cards used in 18th-century textile looms. The people who saw these connections weren't climbing specialized ladders—they were building webs of knowledge that allowed them to see what others missed.

Building a career web requires different skills than climbing a ladder. On a ladder, the primary skills are competition, strategic positioning, and a kind of persistent tunnel vision. In a web, the essential skills are curiosity, relationship-building, pattern recognition, and adaptability.

This doesn't mean the web approach is easy or that it lacks structure. Creating a web still requires intention and effort. But the effort is directed toward exploration and connection rather than just upward movement.

Start small. Identify one adjacent skill or field that genuinely interests you and find a way to explore it. This might mean taking on a side project at work, volunteering for a cross-functional team, or simply having regular coffee with someone in a department you know little about. The goal isn't to become an expert overnight but to begin creating new nodes in your web.

The open-source software community provides a fascinating example of web building in action. In traditional corporate environments, programmers might compete fiercely to climb the ladder—to become senior developers, then team leads, then managers. But in open-source communities, contributors often create value by connecting disparate projects and bringing techniques from one domain to another.

Linus Torvalds, creator of Linux, didn't rise to prominence by climbing a corporate ladder. He built a web of collaboration that now powers much of the world's technology infrastructure. Linux succeeded not because of rigid hierarchy but because its web structure allowed for distributed intelligence and unexpected innovation.

What's most liberating about the web mindset is that it reframes the idea of career "mistakes." In ladder thinking, any sideways move or detour is a failure. In web thinking, these apparent detours often become crucial connections—the very things that give your career resilience and uniqueness.

Nicole spent seven years pursuing a career as a concert violinist before realizing the classical music world wasn't for her. In ladder thinking, those years were "wasted time." She should have been climbing a more practical ladder. But when she moved into arts administration, then into nonprofit management, those years of musical training became invaluable assets. She understood artists in a way her colleagues couldn't. She had performance experience that made her a compelling public speaker. Her web was stronger precisely because it included this supposed "detour."

The web approach also reframes how we think about our relationships. In ladder world, relationships are often transactional—people are valuable to us if they can help us climb. In web world, we recognize that meaningful connections across different domains enrich our work and lives in ways that can't be plotted on a career trajectory.

Economist Brian Arthur once noted that the economy is increasingly driven by what he calls "increasing returns"—situations where value grows exponentially through networks and connections rather than linearly through traditional production. The same is true for careers. In a networked world, the value of your career grows not just through steady "climbing" but through the unexpected synergies between different parts of your web.

This shift from ladder to web thinking might be the most important career change you can make—and it's available to you regardless of your age, background, or current position. Whether you're just starting out or decades into your working life, you can begin weaving a more interconnected, resilient career pattern today.

Ask yourself: What parts of my current work give me energy? What adjacent skills or fields am I curious about? Who in my existing network comes from a completely different background than mine? What would happen if I allowed myself to explore sidewise rather than always upward?

Building a web doesn't mean abandoning ambition or growth. It means redefining what growth looks like. It means recognizing that the richest careers aren't just measured by title or salary but by the breadth of experiences, the depth of relationships, and the unique pattern of contributions that only you can make.

This isn't just idealism. In our rapidly changing world, the web approach is increasingly practical. Industries disappear overnight. New fields emerge just as quickly. The person who has built a diverse web of skills, relationships, and experiences will navigate these shifts far more successfully than the one who has only climbed a single ladder.

Maya, a former pharmaceutical researcher, learned this firsthand when her company closed its R&D division. Her colleagues who had focused solely on climbing the research ladder struggled to reinvent themselves. But Maya had built a web. She had cultivated relationships with marketing teams, learned about regulatory affairs, and developed a side interest in science communication. When research jobs disappeared, she slid smoothly into medical writing—a field that utilized her scientific knowledge while drawing on her communication skills.

The web approach even changes how we view competition. In ladder world, there's only so much room at the top. Your success often comes at someone else's expense. In web world, connections multiply possibilities. Your unique combination of skills and experiences means you're not fighting for the exact same position as anyone else. You're creating value in the spaces between established domains.

This doesn't mean you won't encounter competition or that all career paths are equally viable. It does mean that you have more options than the narrow channel a ladder provides. It means you can create opportunities where none previously existed by combining elements in your web in novel ways.

The greatest freedom in abandoning the ladder is emotional. When you're climbing a ladder, you're always aware of where you stand relative to others. There's always someone above you, someone whose position you envy.

There's always the anxiety of whether you're climbing fast enough. The web doesn't eliminate ambition, but it transforms it from a comparative exercise to a creative one.

Your satisfaction comes not from outclimbing others but from weaving a pattern that reflects who you truly are. The question shifts from "How high can I climb?" to "What unique connections can I create?" It's a subtle shift, but one that can transform work from a source of constant status anxiety to a canvas for genuine contribution.

So screw the ladder. Build a web. Let your career expand outward as well as upward. Create connections between your various interests and skills. Cultivate relationships across different domains. Embrace the detours and the apparent dead ends as potential growth points in your web.

The ladder promises simplicity and clarity—a straight path to some mythical top. The web offers something messier but far more valuable: the chance to create a working life that truly belongs to you, resilient enough to weather change, expansive enough to accommodate growth, and unique enough to express who you really are.

Your career isn't a ladder to climb. It's a web to weave. And only you can determine its pattern.

9 - Restlessness Is a Clue, Not a Curse

You've felt it before. That peculiar itch beneath your skin. The slight but persistent dissatisfaction with your current path. The wandering eye toward other possibilities. The nagging sense that something isn't quite aligned. Most people call it restlessness, and most people treat it like an inconvenience—a bug in our otherwise rational operating system.

What if they're wrong? What if restlessness isn't a glitch but a feature—not a curse to be medicated away but a compass pointing toward something important?

Our culture has a strange relationship with restlessness. We simultaneously glorify and pathologize it. We celebrate the restless innovators who changed the world but medicate our own restlessness with Netflix, alcohol, and endless scrolling. We admire the wanderers in literature but worry about the wanderer in the mirror.

The truth about restlessness lives in a more nuanced territory than our binary thinking allows. Restlessness is neither purely constructive nor destructive—it's informational. And like any form of information, its value depends entirely on how you receive it, interpret it, and respond to it.

I remember reading about Darwin's voyage on the HMS Beagle. Before embarking on what would become his life-defining journey, Darwin was a restless young man who had abandoned medical studies and was drifting through divinity school without much conviction. His father worried he would amount to nothing. But Darwin's restlessness—his inability to settle into conventional paths—wasn't a character flaw. It was the intuitive knowledge that he hadn't yet found where his unique curiosities and abilities could truly flourish.

The opportunity to join the Beagle's expedition came almost by chance. And yet, that restlessness—that inability to feel at home in the paths others had prescribed—ultimately led to the theory of evolution, one of the most profound scientific contributions in human history.

The curious thing about stories like Darwin's is how we tend to interpret them only in retrospect, after success has blessed the restlessness with meaning. We're much less charitable with everyday restlessness—our own or others'—when the outcome remains uncertain.

But restlessness deserves more respect than we give it. Evolutionary psychologists suggest that curiosity and novelty-seeking—close cousins of restlessness—served crucial evolutionary functions. Humans who occasionally wandered beyond the familiar found new resources, new territories, new possibilities. The very human trait of neophilia—love of the new—drove our species to explore every corner of this planet.

So when that restlessness visits you in the quiet moments between tasks, or in the middle of the night when you can't sleep, or during a perfectly pleasant weekend when you should be content but somehow aren't—listen to it. Not with dread or frustration, but with curiosity. What is this ancient evolutionary signal trying to tell you?

Sometimes restlessness whispers of genuine misalignment—work that doesn't engage your abilities, relationships that don't nourish your spirit, or surroundings that don't inspire your creativity. Other times, it speaks of internal shifts—you've grown, but your life hasn't grown with you. You've evolved beyond what once fit perfectly.

Yet people often treat their restlessness as something to overcome rather than something to understand. They push it down, rationalize it away, or distract themselves until it subsides temporarily. This pattern repeats until the whisper of restlessness becomes a shout—manifesting as a midlife crisis, burnout, or depression.

What makes this tendency particularly tragic is that restlessness, properly engaged, can be the beginning of renewal rather than crisis. The most powerful reinventions often begin with a period of healthy restlessness—a sense that something needs to change before you even know what that something is.

Neuroscientist and author Daniel Levitin notes in his research that our brains are actually designed to seek novelty at regular intervals. The neurochemical dopamine, which motivates us to pursue rewards, reacts more strongly to unexpected rewards than predictable ones. This suggests our brains are wired to occasionally shake things up—not out of destructive impulse, but to maintain our capacity for engagement and learning.

Across history, many who changed careers midstream didn't do so because they had a blinding moment of clarity about their true calling. They simply honored their restlessness enough to take a step in a new direction, then another, then another.

Take the case of Martha Graham, who didn't begin serious dance training until her late teens—ancient by ballet standards—and didn't create her revolutionary dance company until her mid-thirties. Her restlessness with conventional movement led her to develop an entirely new language of modern dance that transformed the art form.

Or consider Julia Child, who worked in advertising and later intelligence during World War II before discovering her passion for French cooking at age 36. By following her curiosity rather than dismissing it as inconvenient midlife restlessness, she revolutionized American home cooking and became a cultural icon.

These aren't just cherry-picked success stories; they represent a pattern. Reinvention often begins not with certainty but with discomfort—with the courage to take restlessness seriously without knowing exactly where it leads.

The modern world, however, has little patience for this kind of uncertain exploration. We're expected to know our "personal brand" by our twenties, to build "portable skills" that transcend industries, to be simultaneously specialized and adaptable. The message is clear: Decide early, commit fully, and if you must pivot, do it strategically and quickly.

No wonder so many feel trapped. We've created a culture where the natural human rhythm of curiosity, exploration, restlessness, and renewal has been compressed into an efficient but joyless algorithm. We've pathologized the very impulses that make us human.

Perhaps the most insidious myth about restlessness is that it represents a lack of gratitude or contentment. How often have you felt guilty for wanting something different when your current situation is perfectly "fine"? How many times have you silenced your restlessness with admonishments to appreciate what you have?

But restlessness and gratitude aren't mutually exclusive. You can be deeply thankful for your present circumstances while still honoring the soft voice that says, "There's something more for you to discover." Contentment isn't stasis; it's alignment. And sometimes realignment is necessary as you evolve.

Behavioral economist Dan Ariely's research on decision-making offers another useful lens for understanding restlessness. Ariely has studied how we make choices and found that we often feel more satisfied not when we make perfect decisions but when we feel we've adequately explored our options. In other words, the route to contentment sometimes requires periods of exploration and even restlessness.

This is where the concept of "nudge theory" becomes relevant to our relationship with restlessness. Developed by Richard Thaler and Cass Sunstein, nudge theory suggests that small interventions can help people make better choices without restricting their freedom. Applied to restlessness, this means you don't have to overhaul your entire life at the first sign of dissatisfaction. Small experiments—nudges in new directions—can help you gather data about what might bring better alignment.

Rather than quitting your job the moment restlessness strikes, you might take a class in a subject that intrigues you. Rather than moving cities, you might explore a different neighborhood on weekends. Rather than ending a relationship, you might introduce new shared experiences. These nudges honor your restlessness without requiring drastic action before you understand what it's telling you.

I once read about a corporate lawyer who felt increasingly restless in her high-paying but soul-draining job. Rather than immediately quitting (which would have been financially reckless), she volunteered at a hospital one evening per week. That small nudge eventually revealed her interest in healthcare, leading her to transition to health policy work—a field that utilized her legal expertise but aligned better with her values. Her restlessness wasn't telling her to abandon everything; it was pointing toward a meaningful pivot.

The beauty of treating restlessness as information rather than affliction is that it transforms uncertainty from something to fear into something to explore. When you frame your restlessness as a clue rather than a curse, you approach it with curiosity instead of resistance.

This shift in perspective changes everything. Questions replace commands. "What is this restlessness telling me?" replaces "I need to get rid of this feeling." "What small experiment might help me understand this better?" replaces "What drastic change will make this go away?"

And here's where many people get stuck: they believe that to honor their restlessness, they must have clarity about the destination. But that's backward. Clarity doesn't precede action; it emerges from it. You don't need to see the entire path to take the first step. You just need enough light to see the next few feet ahead.

The novelist E.L. Doctorow once said that writing a novel is like driving at night—you can only see as far as your headlights, but you can make the whole trip that way. The same applies to navigating periods of restlessness. You don't need the full blueprint; you just need to illuminate the next step.

This approach requires humility. It requires admitting that you don't have all the answers, that your life is a work in progress, that your identity is fluid rather than fixed. But within that humility lies tremendous freedom—the freedom to evolve without explanation, to explore without apology, to honor your restlessness as the voice of your becoming rather than a disruption to be silenced.

In her less-known but remarkable book "Gift from the Sea," Anne Morrow Lindbergh writes of life's cyclical nature: "Perhaps this is the most important thing for me to take back from beach-living: simply the memory that each cycle of the tide is valid; each cycle of the wave is valid; each cycle of a relationship is valid." Her wisdom applies equally to our cycles of contentment and restlessness. Each has its purpose, its validity, its gift.

When we fight against our restlessness, we often prolong it. When we embrace it as information—as a clue to something important—we can move through it more gracefully, extracting its wisdom without getting stuck in its discomfort.

The next time restlessness visits you, try greeting it differently. Instead of seeing it as an unwelcome guest, treat it as a messenger carrying news from your deeper self. Sit with it. Listen to it. Ask what it's trying to tell you. The answers may not come immediately or clearly, but the very act of listening changes your relationship with the feeling.

And remember that restlessness doesn't always mean you need a dramatic life overhaul. Sometimes it simply points to neglected aspects of yourself that need expression. The accountant who feels restless might not need to quit his job but might need to make space for his long-abandoned love of painting. The parent consumed by caregiving might not need a new family but might need to reclaim some independence and identity beyond parenting.

Restlessness is rarely about a single life domain; it's about the ecology of your life—the balance between giving and receiving, work and play, connection and solitude, security and risk, familiarity and novelty. When the ecology falls out of balance, restlessness arrives as the ecosystem's way of seeking equilibrium.

So perhaps the most useful response to restlessness isn't to immediately change everything but to ask: What's out of balance? What part of me is being starved? What values am I compromising? What expression am I denying?

The paradox of restlessness is that fighting against it only intensifies it, while moving toward it—with curiosity rather than judgment—often dissolves its more painful aspects, transforming uncomfortable restlessness into purposeful momentum.

The wisdom traditions of nearly every culture recognize this truth. The Tao Te Ching speaks of accomplishing great things by taking small actions. The I Ching honors times of standstill as necessary for renewal. Indigenous wisdom reveres seasonal cycles of activity and rest.

Yet modern culture has little tolerance for fallow periods, for uncertainty, for the "not-knowing" that precedes new growth. We rush to fill empty spaces, to quiet restless feelings, to arrive at certainty before the journey of discovery has properly begun.

What might change if we collectively reimagined restlessness not as a problem to solve but as a natural part of being human—as essential to growth as hunger is to nourishment?

Perhaps we would be gentler with ourselves during periods of uncertainty. Perhaps we would create more spacious lives with room for evolution and reinvention. Perhaps we would judge others less harshly for their midlife career changes, their gap years, their sabbaticals, their periods of questioning.

Your restlessness is not a character flaw. It's not a sign of ingratitude. It's not an indictment of your choices thus far. It's simply information—vital information about the growing edge between who you have been and who you are becoming.

Listen to it. Not obsessively, not desperately, but attentively. Let it be a clue that guides you, not a curse that haunts you. Trust that within its discomfort lies the seed of your next becoming—not because restlessness itself is the goal, but because the authentic life toward which it points is worth the journey.

10 - What You Notice When You're Not Trying to Impress Anyone

There's a peculiar freedom that arrives when you finally stop performing. I don't mean on stage or in front of a camera—I mean the everyday performance we put on for others, the constant awareness of being watched and evaluated. The exhausting vigilance of monitoring how we're perceived.

Most of our lives run on this hidden operating system of impression management. We choose careers that sound impressive at dinner parties. We pursue goals because they make us look successful rather than because they genuinely interest us. We chase achievements that can be displayed on résumés and social media profiles. And in this constant performance, we often lose track of what actually matters to us when no one is watching.

I wonder what would happen if you dropped the script entirely. If you stopped trying to curate a narrative about your life that others would admire. If you allowed yourself to notice what actually catches your attention when status and perception aren't part of the equation.

The most human parts of us often hide in these unguarded moments. The curiosities we don't advertise. The activities we love but never mention because they don't sound impressive enough. The thoughts we have when we're alone that never make it into conversation because they don't fit our carefully constructed personas.

These "unsellable" parts of ourselves—the ones that don't translate neatly into professional bios or Instagram captions—might actually be the most important clues to finding your way.

The anthropologist Claude Lévi-Strauss once said, "The wise man doesn't give the right answers, he poses the right questions." When we're caught in the grip of career indecision or purpose-hunting, we're usually fixated on finding answers. The perfect job. The ideal mission. The life path that will finally feel right. But perhaps wisdom lies in a shift of attention—away from answers and toward the questions that naturally arise when the pressure to impress fades away.

What do you repeatedly return to, not because anyone is watching, but simply because it draws you back? What conversations make you lose track of time? What topics do you read about voluntarily, when there's no external reward?

The psychoanalyst D.W. Winnicott developed a concept he called the "true self" versus the "false self." The false self is essentially a social construct—the persona we develop to navigate the expectations of others. It's not inherently bad; we all need social adaptations. But when the false self overwhelms the true self, we lose contact with our authentic inclinations and desires. We become strangers to ourselves, expertly performing roles while feeling hollow inside.

In 1998, a computer programmer named Brad Fitzpatrick created a small project called LiveJournal—originally just to keep in touch with his high school friends. He wasn't trying to start a company or become a tech celebrity. He was scratching his own itch, following a genuine interest. That personal project ended up revolutionizing blogging platforms and online communities, eventually hosting millions of users. But its origin wasn't strategic or performative—it was someone following their natural curiosity without an audience in mind.

This pattern repeats across domains. The fashion designer Rei Kawakubo of Comme des Garçons didn't train formally in fashion. She simply began making clothes she herself wanted to wear—strange, architecturally interesting garments that defied convention. She wasn't trying to impress the fashion establishment; she was following an internal aesthetic compass. Today, she's considered one of the most influential designers in the world.

These stories aren't meant to promise you fame or success if you follow your unguarded interests. That would just be replacing one form of performative ambition with another. Rather, they illustrate how our most honest inclinations—the ones that exist independent of others' validation—often lead to work that has integrity and staying power.

What might you notice about yourself if you paid attention to when you feel most alive and engaged, regardless of whether those moments fit into your professional narrative or impress others?

Maybe you'd notice that you come alive when explaining complex ideas to others, but have pursued a career where teaching isn't part of your role. Maybe you'd realize that you deeply enjoy solving practical, hands-on problems, yet have channeled yourself into theoretical work because it seemed more prestigious. Or perhaps you'd discover that your natural creativity emerges most when you're collaborating closely with others, yet you've chosen isolated work because it aligns with your self-image as an independent thinker.

The sociologist Erving Goffman wrote extensively about what he called "impression management"—the work we do to control how others perceive us. In his seminal book "The Presentation of Self in Everyday Life," he analyzed how much energy humans expend on maintaining their social personas. This labor isn't just occasional; it's constant, exhausting, and often unconscious. We're continuously adjusting our speech, our posture, our expressions to match the expectations of those around us.

Performative ambition operates on the same principle but at a larger scale. It's not just about managing impressions in the moment—it's about constructing an entire life trajectory around what will garner respect, admiration, or envy from others. It's choosing a college major because it sounds impressive, taking a job because the company name will look good on your resume, pursuing goals you can humbly-brag about on social media.

This performative approach to life choices isn't just exhausting—it's a recipe for disconnection from yourself. If your compass is always oriented toward external validation, you'll never develop the internal navigation system necessary for making choices that actually fit who you are.

There's a surprising freedom in becoming unimpressive. Not in the sense of deliberately sabotaging yourself or embracing mediocrity, but in releasing the constant need to translate your life into status symbols that others will recognize and admire.

The psychiatrist Carl Jung spoke of individuation—the process of becoming more fully yourself by integrating all parts of your personality, including those that don't conform to social expectations. This process requires periods of turning inward, away from the collective values and toward your own nature. It means developing what Jung called "psychological independence"—the ability to discern your own desires from those implanted by family, culture, and society.

This independence doesn't happen automatically. It requires intentional practice in noticing your authentic responses before they're filtered through the lens of "how will this look to others?"

There's a little-known experimental theater technique developed by acting teacher Viola Spolin called "the private moment." Actors practice performing everyday activities as if absolutely no one is watching—as if they're completely alone. The goal is to access behavior that isn't performative, to find the quality of movement and emotion that emerges when the awareness of an audience disappears. It's surprisingly difficult. Most people, even when physically alone, maintain an internal audience—imagining how they appear, maintaining a persona even in solitude.

What would it look like to practice "private moments" in your own life? To create space where your choices aren't immediately translated into their social value? To notice what interests you when no one will ever know about it?

A friend once told me about a former colleague who had been a successful corporate attorney for twenty years. One day, during a routine physical, his doctor asked him about stress relief activities. The lawyer admitted he had none—just work, family obligations, and sleep. The doctor suggested he find something, anything, that he enjoyed purely for itself. Something with no professional application or status value.

After weeks of consideration, the lawyer remembered that as a child, he'd loved building intricate structures with toothpicks. On a whim, he bought some toothpicks and glue. He began spending thirty minutes each evening building tiny architectural models. No one saw them. He didn't photograph them for social media. He didn't mention them to colleagues. Often, he would dismantle them after completion. The activity served no purpose beyond the absorption and pleasure it provided.

Within months, this seemingly insignificant practice had transformed his relationship to his work and his sense of self. By having one area of his life completely free from external evaluation, he remembered what it felt like to act from intrinsic motivation. This small private joy became a touchstone, reminding him of who he was beyond his professional identity and social role.

This story isn't about toothpicks. It's about creating space where your actions aren't immediately converted into their social currency—where you can notice what naturally engages you when the performance pressure is off.

The Swiss psychiatrist Alice Miller wrote about how many of us develop what she called a "false self" in childhood—a persona designed to earn love and approval by being "good," "successful," or "special" according to others' definitions. This false self can be so convincing that we mistake it for who we actually are. We pursue its goals and meet its standards without realizing we're living someone else's idea of a worthy life.

Breaking free from this pattern requires developing what psychologists call "intrinsic motivation"—doing things because they inherently satisfy you rather than because they lead to external rewards or validation. Research shows that people who are primarily driven by intrinsic motivation not only report greater well-being but often produce more creative and substantive work over time. When you're not distracted by how you're being perceived, you can give your full attention to the task itself.

The irony is that some of the most admired and influential work in history came from people who weren't primarily concerned with impressing others. They were absorbed in questions or problems that genuinely fascinated them. Their ambition wasn't performative but intrinsic—driven by curiosity, challenge, or the desire to solve problems they personally cared about.

In the early 1980s, radio producer Ira Glass spent years experimenting with unconventional storytelling formats, not because they would win awards or attract large audiences (initially, they didn't), but because he was genuinely interested in finding new ways to structure narrative journalism. This private creative obsession eventually led to the creation of "This American Life"—one of the most influential radio programs and podcasts in broadcasting history. But its genesis wasn't strategic or audience-focused; it was someone following their own aesthetic curiosity.

What gets in the way of this kind of authentic attention? Often, it's not just external pressure but our own internalized audience—the imagined judges we carry within us. We anticipate criticism before it happens. We filter our genuine interests through the lens of "what will others think?" We self-censor before we've even fully acknowledged our own desires.

Becoming aware of this internal censorship is the first step toward more authentic choices. When a genuine interest or curiosity arises, notice how quickly your mind jumps to evaluating its social worth. Does this make sense for my career? Will people think this is a waste of time? Shouldn't I be doing something more productive?

These evaluative thoughts aren't inherently bad—practical considerations matter. But when they immediately overrule your natural inclinations before you've even had a chance to explore them, you lose the very information you need to make meaningful choices.

The philosopher Martin Heidegger wrote about what he called "authentic existence" versus "inauthentic existence." In inauthentic existence, we make choices based on conformity and convention—doing what "one" does, following established paths without questioning whether they fit our unique situation. Authentic existence, by contrast, involves recognizing that you alone must take responsibility for your choices—that no external authority can tell you how to live your particular life.

This doesn't mean rejecting all social norms or responsibilities. Rather, it means engaging with them consciously rather than automatically—choosing which conventions serve your authentic development and which divert you from it.

The psychologist Mihaly Csikszentmihalyi spent decades studying what he called "flow states"—those moments of complete absorption when you're so engaged in an activity that self-consciousness disappears. In flow, you're not thinking about how you appear or what others might think—you're fully present with the task itself. Csikszentmihalyi's research found that these states of unselfconscious engagement are consistently associated with higher levels of fulfillment and meaning.

What activities reliably induce this state for you? When do you become so absorbed that you forget to check your phone, lose track of time, and stop monitoring how you appear? These flow-producing activities often contain important information about what genuinely engages your attention and abilities.

Sometimes the most powerful clues about your path come not from what impresses others but from what you find yourself doing when no external reward is offered. What do you read about voluntarily? What problems do you solve for fun? What activities would you continue even if you received no recognition for them?

Author Neil Gaiman tells a story about imposter syndrome and finding his authentic path. Early in his career, after some initial success, he was invited to a gathering of famous artists and writers. Feeling out of place, he mentioned to an elderly gentleman that he felt like a fraud who didn't belong there. The man—who turned out to be celebrated science fiction author Isaac Asimov—told him, "Everyone here feels like that. But you're here because you're doing something that only you can do."

This gets at something essential: the path that's truly yours isn't the one that impresses the most people—it's the one that allows you to contribute something that emerges from your particular configuration of interests, experiences, and abilities. Something that wouldn't exist in quite the same way without you.

Releasing the need to impress doesn't mean abandoning ambition or excellence. Rather, it means redirecting that energy from managing perceptions to developing mastery and contribution that matter to you regardless of their social currency.

What would happen if, just as an experiment, you made one choice today based entirely on what genuinely interests you, with no thought of how it might be perceived? What if you followed that interest a little further tomorrow, and the next day? Not with grand expectations of discovering your life's purpose, but simply to practice noticing what engages you when performance pressure is removed?

The most reliable path through indecision isn't usually a sudden revelation or dramatic change. It's a gradual process of becoming more attuned to your unguarded responses—learning to recognize the subtle pull of genuine interest beneath the louder voices of should's and expectations.

When you're not busy trying to impress anyone, you might finally hear the quieter voice of your own curiosity. And in that honest attention, you might discover not the perfect path, but your path—the one that feels like walking toward yourself rather than away from who you truly are.

11 - Being Average is Not an Insult

The first time someone called me average, I felt the sting of it for days. Average. Ordinary. Unremarkable. In a world that worships at the altar of exceptionalism, these words land like insults, like accusations of wasted potential.

But what if we've got it all backward? What if average isn't an insult, but an invitation?

We live in the age of the highlight reel. Social media has turned everyday life into a competition where the prize is attention and the entry fee is constant striving. The message hammered into us from childhood is clear: be extraordinary or be forgotten. Excel or be invisible. Stand out or stand aside.

Yet beneath this collective hunger for recognition lies an uncomfortable truth: most of us, by definition, are average at most things we do. And that's not just okay—it might be the secret to a well-lived life.

Take a moment to imagine something revolutionary: pursuing an activity with no expectation of mastery, with no dreams of acclaim, with no desire to monetize it or build a personal brand around it. Just doing something because it brings you joy, even if you never rise above the middle of the pack.

How foreign that feels. How quietly rebellious.

The modern economy has convinced us that anything worth doing is worth doing for profit, for advancement, for some tangible return on investment. Every hobby must become a side hustle. Every interest must be optimized. Every pursuit must contribute to your personal brand, your future earning potential, your marketplace value.

But this commodification of human experience has robbed us of something precious: the simple pleasure of doing things badly.

In 1970s suburban America, there was a phenomenon that now seems almost quaint: adults regularly gathered to do things they weren't particularly good at. They formed amateur bowling leagues and softball teams. They joined community theater productions and church choirs. They took pottery classes and learned to square dance. They painted landscapes that would never hang in galleries and played musical instruments that would never grace concert halls.

And critically, they didn't expect to get better. Their mediocrity wasn't a phase to push through on the path to expertise—it was the whole point. The joy was in the doing, in the togetherness, in the process rather than the product.

Somewhere along the way, we lost this. Now, we download apps that track our progress, that quantify our improvement, that rank us against others. We've transformed activities that once brought simple pleasure into opportunities for optimization. We've made leisure into labor.

A little-known but revealing study from 2017 at the University of Zurich found that when recreational runners began tracking their performance with apps and devices, their reported enjoyment of running decreased significantly over time. The simple act of measurement transformed something liberating into something evaluative. The runners became less present in their bodies and more fixated on their metrics. The joy of movement was replaced by the anxiety of achievement.

This isn't to say that striving for excellence is inherently problematic. The pursuit of mastery can be deeply fulfilling. But when excellence becomes the only acceptable outcome for everything we do, we've created a recipe for perpetual dissatisfaction and narrowed the range of experiences available to us.

The writer Kurt Vonnegut once offered this advice: "Practice any art—music, singing, dancing, acting, drawing, painting, sculpting, poetry, fiction, essays, reportage—no matter how well or badly, not to get money and fame, but to experience becoming, to find out what's inside you, to make your soul grow."

Notice what's missing from this advice: any mention of talent, achievement, or external validation. Vonnegut understood that the value of creative pursuits isn't in the quality of what we produce, but in how the production changes us.

In northern England, there's a remarkable little story that rarely makes it into conversations about meaningful work.

For over forty years, a group called "The Fishburn Band" has met weekly in a small mining town. The band consists mostly of former coal miners, men who spent their working lives in darkness and danger. None had formal musical training. Few could read sheet music when they started. By conventional standards, they weren't particularly good musicians.

But every Thursday evening, they gathered in the town hall with their mismatched instruments—some donated, some salvaged, some purchased secondhand—and they played. They played folk songs and simple arrangements of classical pieces. They played for each other, for their families, for anyone who cared to listen.

When a documentary filmmaker asked one longtime member why he kept coming back decade after decade despite never advancing beyond a basic level of skill, the man looked genuinely confused by the question. "It's Thursday," he said simply. "This is what we do on Thursdays."

There's profound wisdom in that response—a recognition that value doesn't always have to be measured in achievement or improvement. Sometimes, the mere continuity of a practice, the ritual of showing up, the community it creates—these are enough.

Capitalism has trained us to think of ourselves as products in need of constant enhancement, perpetually competing for limited resources and recognition. This mindset has seeped into our leisure time, our creative expressions, our personal relationships. We've internalized the message that if we're not the best, we're nothing.

But what if mediocrity—being solidly in the middle, neither spectacular nor terrible—isn't a failure of ambition but a radical act of self-acceptance?

There's a beautiful psychological concept called "the good-enough parent," developed by pediatrician and psychoanalyst Donald Winnicott in the 1950s. Winnicott observed that children don't need perfect parents to thrive; they need parents who are consistently adequate, who meet basic needs reliably without the pressure of flawlessness. In fact, he argued that "perfect" parenting—which inevitably stems from parental anxiety rather than attunement to the child—actually impedes a child's development.

We might extend this concept beyond parenting to our relationship with ourselves and our pursuits. Perhaps we don't need to be exceptional at everything we do. Perhaps "good enough" isn't settling—it's sustainable.

The Australian philosopher Damon Young writes about the concept of "middling," which he describes as "the courage to be mediocre." This isn't about embracing laziness or rejecting growth. It's about recognizing that our worth isn't contingent on our performance, that our humanity isn't earned through excellence.

Young points out that for most of human history, people did not expect to be extraordinary. They aimed to be decent community members, to master the skills their survival required, to find small pleasures where they could. The burden of potential—this idea that we might become anything, achieve anything, if only we work hard enough—is uniquely modern, and uniquely exhausting.

There's freedom in releasing yourself from the tyranny of potential. There's relief in saying, "I don't need to be the best at this. I don't need to improve at this. I can simply do this because it brings me joy in this moment."

Think of the people you love most deeply. Are they the most talented individuals you've ever met? The most successful? The most productive? Or are they the ones who show up for you consistently, who make you feel seen and valued, who share your days with warmth and presence?

Excellence matters in some contexts, certainly. I want an excellent surgeon if I need an operation. I want excellent engineers designing the bridges I drive across. But do I need an excellent baker to enjoy a homemade cookie? Do I need an excellent singer to appreciate a lullaby? Do I need an excellent gardener to take pleasure in watching something grow?

In 2019, a small study out of the University of Michigan looked at the impact of recreational activities on perceived well-being. The researchers divided participants into two groups: those who engaged in activities with the explicit goal of improvement, and those who engaged in activities with the explicit goal of enjoyment. After six months, the "enjoyment" group reported significantly higher satisfaction with their recreational time, stronger social connections, and—most surprisingly—were more likely to have maintained their practice.

The pursuit of excellence, it seems, can sometimes undermine the very thing that draws us to an activity in the first place.

This isn't an argument for mediocrity in all things. It's an argument for intentional mediocrity in some things—for creating space in your life where the pressure to excel is consciously set aside, where the joy of doing is untethered from the quality of what's done.

When was the last time you did something just because it made you happy, with no expectation that you'd be particularly good at it? When was the last time you allowed yourself to be a beginner without the promise of eventual mastery? When was the last time you valued an experience not for what it might lead to, but for what it was in the moment?

The writer and theologian Frederick Buechner once defined vocation as "the place where your deep gladness and the world's deep hunger meet." This is a beautiful sentiment, but it places a heavy burden on our choices. What if instead of seeking the perfect intersection of passion and purpose, we simply sought experiences that made us more fully human, more present, more alive?

In Japan, there's a tradition called "Bojutsu," or staff fighting. It's an ancient martial art, and like many such practices, it typically takes decades to master. But in some rural communities, there's a different approach. Elderly villagers gather not to perfect their technique or to progress through ranks, but simply to move their bodies in community, to maintain a connection to tradition, to spend time together in purposeful play.

A Western observer might look at these gatherings and see only imperfection—the forms executed without precision, the movements slowed by age. But this view misses everything that matters: the laughter, the shared history, the gentle exercise, the intergenerational bonds formed as younger members join the circle.

This is the beauty of allowing yourself to be average: it shifts your focus from outcome to process, from product to experience, from future validation to present engagement.

Of course, there's a fine line between embracing mediocrity and settling for less than you desire. This isn't permission to abandon pursuits that truly matter to you or to avoid challenges that might lead to growth. It's an invitation to examine your motivations honestly, to distinguish between the things you do for external validation and the things you do for internal satisfaction.

It's about asking: If no one ever saw this, would I still do it? If I knew I would never improve beyond a basic level of competence, would this still bring me joy? If this never led to any tangible reward, would it still feel worthwhile?

These questions cut through the noise of social comparison and touch the heart of authentic desire. They remind us that not everything we do needs to be calibrated for maximum impact or efficiency. Some things can simply be for us, in this moment, imperfect and complete.

The next time someone calls you average, consider the possibility that they've offered not an insult but a release— a reminder that you're human, that you don't have to carry the weight of extraordinary expectations, that you can find profound meaning in ordinary pursuits.

Being average isn't failing to reach your potential. It's recognizing that your worth was never contingent on your performance in the first place. It's remembering that life isn't a competition to die with the most impressive resume.

Perhaps the most remarkable achievement isn't excellence at all, but the courage to do things badly, joyfully, in full view of others—to show up not as the person you might theoretically become with enough effort, but as the person you already are, with all your glorious limitations and your singular capacity for delight.

Average isn't an insult. It's an invitation to put down the measuring stick and pick up whatever calls to you— clumsily, imperfectly, and with complete abandon.

12 - The Inner Scorecard Revisited

How often have you caught yourself checking the likes on your latest post, or rehearsing how you'll tell someone about your recent promotion? We've become so accustomed to documenting our achievements that we sometimes forget to ask whether they matter to us at all. The inner scorecard—a concept borrowed from investment legends Charlie Munger and Warren Buffett—invites us to pause this external validation cycle and ask a deceptively simple question: Would you still do what you're doing if nobody would ever know?

The inner scorecard is deceptively simple: it's the private tally of your life that only you can see and measure. The outer scorecard, by contrast, is the public-facing sum of your accomplishments, accolades, and socially-recognized successes. Most of us spend extraordinary energy managing the latter while neglecting the former.

Buffett often tells students: "Would you rather be the world's greatest lover, but have everyone think you're the world's worst lover? Or would you rather be the world's worst lover but have everyone think you're the world's greatest lover?" After the laughter dies down, he delivers the punchline: "Here's the catch—you have to know the truth about yourself." The quip reveals a profound insight about human nature—we desperately want others to think well of us, even at the expense of our own integrity.

I once met a former hedge fund manager who abandoned a seven-figure income to teach mathematics at a rural high school. When asked why, he didn't launch into platitudes about giving back or finding meaning. Instead, he described the private satisfaction of watching a student grasp a difficult concept, comparing it to the hollow congratulations he received for managing other people's money. "Nobody sees those moments when a kid's face lights up with understanding," he told me, "but they're the only metric that matters to me now." His scorecard had fundamentally changed, becoming invisible to almost everyone but himself.

The tragedy of modern ambition lies not in wanting too much but in wanting the wrong things for the wrong reasons. We've been conditioned to pursue goals that photograph well for social media or sound impressive at cocktail parties. The real estate broker who secretly despises the hustle but loves the status. The academic publishing papers they don't believe in but need for tenure. The entrepreneur building a company they have no passion for because it might lead to a lucrative exit. These are lives guided by outer scorecards—lives that may look successful from the outside while feeling empty from within.

The inner scorecard demands a difficult reckoning because it requires you to define success on your own terms. This is considerably harder than it sounds. We absorb definitions of success from our parents, teachers, peers, and culture long before we develop the capacity to question them. By the time we're adults, these inherited metrics feel like our own, even though they frequently originate elsewhere. Breaking free requires archaeological work—digging through layers of accumulated expectations to uncover what truly resonates with your core self.

A fascinating study from the University of Rochester tracked over 10,000 graduates for two decades, comparing those pursuing "extrinsic goals" (wealth, fame, image) against those pursuing "intrinsic goals" (personal growth, relationships, community). The results were striking: the extrinsically-motivated group achieved more conventional success but reported lower life satisfaction, more depression, and higher anxiety. The intrinsically-motivated group—those with robust inner scorecards—experienced greater overall well-being despite often achieving less recognizable external success.

The most insidious aspect of the outer scorecard is how it shifts with cultural winds. In the 1950s, becoming a loyal company man might have earned social approval. In the 1980s, it was the high-flying corporate raider. By the 2010s, it was the tech entrepreneur disrupting industries. Today, it might be the digital nomad with the perfect Instagram aesthetic. These templates for success change so rapidly that chasing them becomes an exercise in futility— like trying to hit a target that moves every few years.

Where the outer scorecard breeds competition—there are only so many corner offices, viral tweets, or industry awards—the inner scorecard permits infinite winners. Your neighbor's garden doesn't diminish yours; your colleague's sense of purpose doesn't detract from your own. When success becomes personal rather than comparative, we create space for admiration without envy.

The comedian Maria Bamford built her career around deeply personal, sometimes uncomfortable material about mental health, family dynamics, and her own psychiatric hospitalizations. For years, she performed in half-empty clubs to audiences who often didn't know what to make of her unconventional style. Mainstream success eluded her while contemporaries with broader appeal advanced rapidly. Yet she continued refining her unique voice, guided by her own standards of artistic integrity. When asked about this period, she doesn't describe it as suffering or paying dues, but as essential artistic development. "I was doing exactly what I wanted to be doing," she explains, "even when nobody was watching." Her inner scorecard allowed her to recognize success long before external validation arrived.

How do we develop this inner scorecard? It begins with silence. Not the metaphorical kind, but actual quiet—stepping away from the noise of opinions, expectations, and comparisons long enough to hear yourself think. This might mean a digital detox, a solitary weekend, or even just a daily hour without input. The goal is creating space to recognize which pursuits energize you when nobody's watching and which ones drain you even when they impress others.

Try this thought experiment: Imagine you've just died (cheerful, I know), and two ceremonies will be held. The first is your public funeral, where people will speak about your accomplishments and contributions. The second is a private gathering of those who knew you most intimately—perhaps just three or four people—who will speak honestly about who you really were. Would these accounts align or contradict? The gap between these narratives reveals the distance between your inner and outer scorecards.

The psychologist Mihaly Csikszentmihalyi documented thousands of people's experiences of "flow"—that state of complete absorption where time seems to disappear. What's remarkable about flow is that it's often triggered by activities with no external reward. The amateur musician lost in playing a difficult piece, the weekend woodworker shaping a joint, the hiker mesmerized by a mountain trail—these experiences create no measurable outputs for the outer scorecard yet register as deeply meaningful on the inner one.

Yet living exclusively by an inner scorecard presents its own challenges. We're social creatures who need external feedback. The artist needs an audience, the scientist needs peer review, the craftsperson needs clients. Complete disregard for external validation can lead to self-indulgence or disconnection. The sweet spot lies in using the outer scorecard as information while letting the inner scorecard make the final call.

Warren Buffett's business partner Charlie Munger elaborated on this principle beyond investing, describing how his father—a prairie lawyer with modest means—lived by a strict inner scorecard. Despite opportunities to capitalize on his position, the elder Munger refused anything that compromised his standards, even when no one would have known. This integrity didn't make him rich or famous, but it earned him something more valuable— the quiet certainty that he was living according to his own best judgment.

When facing career indecision, we typically ask: "What should I do?" This framing starts with action rather than evaluation. A better question might be: "What would make me proud, even if no one else ever knew about it?" This subtle shift transforms the decision from external considerations (salary, prestige, advancement) to internal ones (growth, integrity, genuine interest).

Imagine, for instance, two paths: one involves developing expertise in a lucrative but personally uninspiring field. The other involves building skill in an area that genuinely interests you but offers more modest rewards. The outer scorecard would likely push you toward the first option. The inner scorecard might favor the second. Neither choice is inherently right or wrong, but making the decision with awareness of which scorecard you're using brings clarity.

The neuroscientist Sam Harris once described anxiety as "the friction between who we are and who we think we should be." When our actions align with our inner scorecard, this friction diminishes. We may still face challenges, setbacks, or difficulties, but they don't threaten our core identity because external outcomes become secondary to internal coherence.

Here's a practical approach: rather than asking whether a choice will lead to success (an outer scorecard question), ask whether it will lead to growth (an inner scorecard question). Success is binary and comparative; you either achieve it or you don't, and it's measured against others. Growth is continuous and personal; it happens regardless of outcome, and it's measured only against yourself.

The folk singer Dave Van Ronk never achieved the commercial success of contemporaries like Bob Dylan, but he maintained an unwavering commitment to artistic authenticity throughout a career spanning nearly fifty years. While the music industry chased trends, Van Ronk stayed true to his eclectic repertoire of blues, jazz, and folk traditions. When asked if he regretted not achieving wider recognition, he responded with characteristic directness: "I've spent my life doing exactly what I wanted to do with exactly the people I wanted to do it with." His inner scorecard rendered the question of "success" almost meaningless.

Sometimes the inner scorecard leads you away from conventional career paths entirely. Consider Patrick Leigh Fermor, who dropped out of school at sixteen and decided to walk across Europe from Holland to Constantinople in the 1930s. This seemingly aimless wandering laid the foundation for his later work as one of the twentieth century's greatest travel writers. Had he followed a traditional outer scorecard, we might have lost the magnificent trilogy that began with "A Time of Gifts"—books that capture not just places but the interior experience of enchantment and discovery.

The act of reclaiming your inner scorecard isn't a one-time decision but an ongoing practice. Society constantly broadcasts metrics of success—income brackets, relationship milestones, career advancement—that can override your internal guidance system if you're not vigilant. The trickiest part is distinguishing between goals you genuinely want and those you've been conditioned to pursue. A useful test: pay attention to how you feel when something goes well. Are you more excited to experience the achievement or to tell others about it? The answer reveals which scorecard is driving you.

Some of history's most contented people were those who implemented ruthlessly honest inner scorecards. The French mathematician Évariste Galois worked through the night before his death in a duel at age twenty, frantically documenting revolutionary mathematical ideas that wouldn't be appreciated for decades. He wasn't writing for fame or recognition—he was responding to an internal imperative to capture what he believed was true and important, regardless of external validation.

When we find ourselves stuck at career crossroads, paralyzed by indecision, the problem often isn't lack of information—it's confusion about which scorecard we're using. The cacophony of external metrics drowns out the quieter voice of our inner accounting. In these moments, try this clarifying question: "If I were the only person who ever knew about this choice, what would I do?" The answer cuts through the noise of expectations and comparisons, revealing what matters to you when all external factors are removed.

The irony of the inner scorecard, of course, is that people who follow it often end up succeeding by outer standards anyway. Their work carries an authenticity that resonates. Their decisions reflect a coherence that inspires trust. Their lives demonstrate an integrity that attracts others. But this success comes as a by-product rather than a goal—and they remain remarkably indifferent to it because they've already achieved what matters most to them: alignment with their own values.

Perhaps the most profound shift that comes with adopting an inner scorecard is how it transforms our relationship with time. When we're chasing external validation, we're perpetually striving for a future moment when we'll finally have "enough" recognition, achievement, or status. With an inner scorecard, the evaluation happens in real-time. You know immediately whether you're acting in accordance with your principles. You feel it when you're growing or stagnating. You don't need to wait for quarterly reviews or social media engagement to tell you if you're on the right track.

So as you navigate the wilderness of career indecision, consider developing your inner scorecard before choosing your direction. Ask what metrics truly matter to you, not the ones that would impress at your class reunion. Define success in terms you can control rather than outcomes subject to luck and circumstance. And remember that the most meaningful accomplishments are often the ones that never make it onto a resume—the small acts of integrity, the quiet moments of mastery, the private victories only you will ever know about.

Because ultimately, you can fool everyone else, but you can't fool your inner scorecard. And at the end of the day, it's the only one that counts.

13 - Don't Make a 10-Year Plan. Make a 10-Week Experiment

There's a particular kind of pain that comes from sitting across from someone who asks, "Where do you see yourself in five years?" Whether it's a job interviewer, a well-meaning relative, or your own reflection in the mirror, the question carries an implicit assumption: that you should know. That somehow, amid the chaos of an unpredictable world, you're supposed to have plotted a detailed map of your future. This expectation isn't just unrealistic—it's fundamentally misaligned with how discovery actually works.

The 10-year plan has become something of a cultural totem, a symbol of ambition and foresight. We're told that successful people chart their courses far in advance, breaking their grand visions into actionable steps with military precision. The problem isn't that long-term planning is inherently bad—it's that it tends to calcify into a rigid structure that can't accommodate the serendipity, curiosity, and spontaneous learning that often leads to our most meaningful work.

What if, instead of plotting distant outcomes, we focused on designing revealing experiments? Small, manageable projects with defined timeframes that help us gather actual data about our interests, aptitudes, and opportunities. Not 10-year commitments, but 10-week experiments.

This isn't merely a semantic shift. It represents a fundamentally different approach to navigating uncertainty. Long-term plans often function as psychological security blankets, giving us the comforting illusion of control. Experiments, by contrast, acknowledge that we don't know what we don't know. They help us discover what lights us up, what we're unexpectedly good at, and what opportunities exist that we couldn't have imagined.

In the 1930s, a group of researchers at Stanford led by Lewis Terman began one of the longest-running psychological studies in history. They tracked over 1,500 intellectually gifted children throughout their lives to see what factors predicted success and fulfillment. One of the most surprising findings was that the participants who rigidly stuck to their early career plans often achieved less than those who remained adaptable and responsive to new opportunities. The children who became the most satisfied and successful adults weren't those with the clearest early vision—they were those who maintained curiosity and openness to unexpected paths.

Our natural impulse when facing uncertainty is to reduce it—to narrow possibilities down to a single, secure path as quickly as possible. But what if uncertainty isn't something to be eliminated but rather a resource to be leveraged? The 10-week experiment embraces uncertainty by creating small, safe spaces to explore without demanding premature commitment.

Take the case of Janice Bryant Howroyd, who founded ActOne Group, now a billion-dollar staffing agency. Her path didn't begin with a grand vision or a detailed business plan. It began with a simple two-month experiment: helping a friend's business place temporary workers. She had $1,500, a phone, and a fax machine. "I didn't have a five-year plan," she's noted in interviews. "I had a day-to-day commitment to see what this could be." That limited experiment provided immediate feedback, revealed unexpected opportunities, and gradually evolved into a multinational enterprise.

The beauty of the 10-week timeframe is that it's long enough to yield meaningful data but short enough to minimize risk. It creates urgency without panic, commitment without entrapment. You can't procrastinate indefinitely when the clock is ticking, but neither are you wed to a path if the experiment reveals it's not for you.

Silicon Valley investor and entrepreneur Peter Thiel often asks founders: "What important truth do very few people agree with you on?" I'd propose this answer: Most paths worth taking don't reveal themselves until you're already moving. The 10-week experiment acknowledges this reality, prioritizing motion over perfect preparation.

In his book "Little Bets," Peter Sims documents how comedian Chris Rock develops his material not through careful planning but through rapid experimentation. Rock appears at small comedy clubs with a notebook, testing dozens of small joke fragments, most of which fail completely. But through this iterative process of rapid experimentation, he gradually identifies and refines the material that resonates. What appears to audiences as a polished Netflix special actually emerged from countless small bets in low-stakes environments.

The psychological benefits of this approach are substantial. Long-term planning often triggers analysis paralysis—the tendency to overthink and overanalyze situations until you're unable to make any decision at all. The experiment model focuses on the next immediate step rather than the entire staircase. It creates forward momentum that often dissolves the very uncertainty that initially felt paralyzing.

There's an obscure gem of a novel called "The Conversationalist" by Ian Frazier that follows a young university graduate who can't decide what to do with his life. Rather than committing to a specific career, he decides to become a "conversationalist"—someone who simply engages people in meaningful dialogue. For three months, he sits in cafes and parks, initiating conversations with strangers. What begins as a peculiar experiment gradually reveals both his natural talents and the unexpected opportunities that arise from genuine human connection. The novel elegantly captures how temporary experiments can reveal permanent insights about ourselves.

The mistake many of us make is confusing experimentation with aimlessness. An experiment is not random motion; it's structured discovery. It has a hypothesis, a timeframe, and measurable outcomes. "I wonder if I'd enjoy working in healthcare" becomes "For the next 10 weeks, I'll volunteer at a hospital for 5 hours weekly and interview three people in different healthcare roles to see what energizes me and what drains me." Specificity transforms vague wondering into actionable learning.

This approach also reconciles two seemingly contradictory pieces of wisdom: "Perseverance is essential" and "Know when to quit." Without the structured timeframe of an experiment, it's difficult to distinguish between necessary persistence and fruitless stubbornness. The experiment creates a natural reflection point where you evaluate what you've learned and decide whether to iterate, expand, or gracefully abandon that particular path.

Modern career trajectories increasingly support this experimental mindset. According to labor statistics, the average worker will have 12 jobs across multiple industries during their lifetime. This isn't because people lack commitment—it's because the economy itself has become more fluid. Industries emerge and transform too rapidly for rigid 10-year plans to remain relevant. Small experiments allow you to gather actionable intelligence about this changing landscape without betting your entire future on a single path.

One of the more fascinating case studies in experimental career development comes from the unlikeliest of places—professional skateboarding. Rodney Mullen, widely considered the most influential street skateboarder in history, developed his approach through what he calls "micro-failures." Rather than planning elaborate routines, he would spend hours attempting simple variations—slightly adjusting foot position, changing timing, or modifying balance points. These tiny experiments, each lasting just minutes, eventually led to innovations that transformed the entire sport. "The secret to creativity," Mullen has said, "is knowing how to hide your sources." His approach wasn't about grand vision but about relentless, playful experimentation.

The 10-week experiment works because it aligns with how our brains naturally learn. Cognitive scientists have demonstrated that we develop expertise not through abstract planning but through direct experience with rapid feedback loops. The more quickly we can test our assumptions against reality, the faster we develop both skills and clarity. Long-term plans often delay this essential feedback, leaving us to operate on untested assumptions about what we'll enjoy or excel at.

When applied to career indecision, the experimental approach offers particular benefits. Instead of the binary "pick a path" approach, it creates a middle ground where multiple directions can be explored simultaneously or sequentially. Curious about both writing and data science? Run two 10-week experiments—one where you write daily and share your work online, another where you take on a small data analysis project. The insights from these parallel tracks often cross-pollinate in unexpected ways.

Not all experiments need to be career-focused. Some of the most revealing experiments involve testing different environments, working styles, or collaborative arrangements. A person might discover they produce their best work in early morning solitude, or that they thrive in collaborative settings with rapid feedback. These meta-experiments about process can be as valuable as those about specific domains or industries.

The stand-up comedian Hannah Gadsby began performing not as a carefully planned career move but as a brief experiment prompted by a friend's dare. She entered a comedy competition with no expectation beyond surviving the experience. That single experiment led to others, gradually revealing not just her talent for comedy but her unique perspective that ultimately redefined what stand-up could be. Her groundbreaking special "Nanette" wouldn't exist if she hadn't taken that initial experimental step.

What makes the 10-week timeframe particularly powerful is that it's long enough to push through the initial discomfort of trying something new. Most new endeavors involve an awkward phase where our skills don't yet match our taste or expectations. This gap—between what we can currently produce and what we can recognize as good—causes many people to abandon promising paths prematurely. The structured timeframe of an experiment helps us commit to pushing through this uncomfortable phase, often revealing aptitudes and interests that would otherwise remain hidden.

The experimental mindset also changes how we relate to failure. In a traditional planning framework, deviations from the expected path feel like failures. In an experimental framework, unexpected outcomes are simply data—valuable information that informs the next iteration.

This perspective shift doesn't just make setbacks more bearable; it actually extracts more learning from them.

John Wooden, the legendary UCLA basketball coach, embodied this principle with his teams. Rather than focusing primarily on season-long goals, he structured practices around what were essentially micro-experiments—testing specific plays, defensive arrangements, or player combinations. Each practice became a laboratory for discovery rather than merely a step toward a predetermined outcome. This approach led to an unprecedented 10 NCAA championships in 12 years. The long-term success emerged not from rigid adherence to a master plan but from a series of revealing experiments and the willingness to adapt based on what they revealed.

To begin applying this approach, start by identifying areas of genuine curiosity—not what you think you should be interested in, but what actually draws your attention. Convert these curiosities into concrete experiments with specific activities and timeframes. "I'm interested in graphic design" becomes "For the next 10 weeks, I'll complete one design tutorial each week and create a portfolio piece based on what I learn." The specificity creates accountability, while the limited timeframe prevents both procrastination and premature commitment.

Document your experiments. Keep notes not just on what you're doing but on your emotional responses throughout the process. Which aspects energize you? Which drain you? What surprises you? These notes become invaluable data for designing future experiments and identifying patterns across different domains. The goal isn't just to test specific careers but to discover the underlying elements that bring you alive.

Perhaps most importantly, maintain a curious mindset throughout. The most valuable experiments often reveal insights we weren't even looking for. The graphic design experiment might reveal not a passion for design itself but for solving visual communication problems. The hospital volunteering might show that you thrive in crisis situations but struggle with routine care. These unexpected discoveries often point to deeper patterns that can guide future experiments and eventually lead to meaningful work.

Some of the most consequential experiments don't look like experiments at all. They're simply periods of deliberate attention to activities you're already engaged in. The software engineer who notices she most enjoys explaining technical concepts to non-technical colleagues. The accountant who finds unexpected satisfaction in organizing community events. These observations can become the seeds of intentional experiments to expand these energizing elements.

The writer and biochemist Isaac Asimov, known for his prolific output across multiple genres, didn't begin with a master plan for his career. He followed what he called "controlled drift"—a series of experiments in different forms of writing, from science fiction to popular science to mysteries. Each new direction emerged not from long-term planning but from curiosity about where a particular interest might lead if explored for a defined period. This experimental approach led to over 500 books across multiple fields—an output that no single master plan could have conceived.

The 10-week experiment framework offers a middle path between rigid planning and aimless wandering. It provides structure without confinement, direction without premature commitment. It acknowledges that most meaningful careers aren't discovered through abstract contemplation but through active engagement with the world. We find our paths by walking them, by testing hypotheses about ourselves and our potential contributions.

So the next time someone asks about your five-year plan, perhaps the most honest and useful answer is: "I'm currently running an experiment to gather data about that very question." Because ultimately, the people who find the most meaningful work aren't those who plan their futures with military precision. They're the ones who design revealing experiments, pay attention to the results, and follow the trail of curiosity and competence wherever it leads.

The 10-week experiment isn't just a technique—it's a philosophy that values discovery over prediction, curiosity over certainty, and adaptation over rigid adherence to plans. It recognizes that in a world of increasing complexity and change, the ability to design good experiments may be more valuable than the ability to formulate perfect plans. It suggests that perhaps the best way to predict your future is to create small pieces of it, right now, and see what they reveal.

14 - You Don't Have to Be Useful All the Time

Somewhere along the way, we began measuring our lives in output. The question "What did you do today?" became the unspoken metric of whether the day was worth living. Productivity became our secular religion, with its own rituals, prophets, and promises of salvation through efficiency. We worship at the altar of usefulness, convinced that our value lies in what we produce rather than who we are. This belief runs so deep that many of us feel a peculiar guilt when we find ourselves momentarily untethered from purpose—as if existing without immediate utility is some kind of moral failure.

The insidious thing about this mindset isn't just that it's exhausting (though it certainly is that). It's that it fundamentally misunderstands what makes a human life meaningful and sustainable. Our obsession with constant productivity is relatively new in human history, yet we've internalized it so completely that we barely question its premises. What if usefulness isn't the highest virtue? What if periods of apparent uselessness are not just acceptable but essential to a well-lived life?

This isn't an argument for laziness or neglecting responsibilities. It's a reconsideration of the relationship between doing and being, between production and restoration, between usefulness and value. Because the truth—which we know intuitively but often forget consciously—is that you don't have to be useful all the time.

The expectation of perpetual productivity runs counter to everything we know about human biology. Our bodies operate according to natural rhythms and cycles—daily circadian rhythms, monthly hormonal cycles, seasonal variations in energy. These aren't design flaws to be overcome; they're sophisticated regulatory systems developed over millions of years of evolution. When we override these rhythms in service of constant output, we're essentially running our biological machinery against its specifications.

An emerging body of neuroscience research reveals the critical importance of what scientists call the "default mode network"—a constellation of brain regions that activate when we're not focused on external tasks. For years, researchers dismissed this as the brain's "resting state." But recent studies show it's actually a period of crucial cognitive processing—memory consolidation, identity construction, emotional regulation, and moral reasoning. When we never step away from active productivity, we literally prevent our brains from performing some of their most important functions.

The poet and philosopher David Whyte speaks of "the conversational nature of reality"—the idea that life unfolds not through our monologues of intention and effort, but through an ongoing dialogue between what we plan and what the world offers back. Constant productivity is essentially a refusal to listen to the other half of the conversation. It's all output, no input. All talking, no listening. All doing, no receiving.

This imbalance shows up with striking clarity in the research of leisure studies scholar Ben Hunnicutt, who documented the strange trajectory of American attitudes toward work and leisure over the past century. In the early 1900s, economists widely predicted that increasing productivity would lead to a significant reduction in working hours. As technology made us more efficient, they reasoned, we would need less time to meet our material needs, freeing us for leisure, community, and creativity.

Instead, something curious happened. As productivity increased, rather than maintaining the same output with less effort, we chose to produce exponentially more. Work hours didn't dramatically decrease; they just yielded more goods and services. Rather than using our technological prowess to create more space for contemplation, connection, and rest, we doubled down on production. Productivity became not a means to an end but an end in itself.

The language we use reveals this shift. We talk about "spending" time rather than "passing" it. We "use" hours rather than experience them. Time becomes a resource to be exploited rather than a dimension to be inhabited. Even our leisure often carries the burden of utility—exercise for health outcomes, hobbies that might become side hustles, rest that's justified only as recovery for more work.

This mindset breeds what philosopher Byung-Chul Han calls "the burnout society"—a culture so fixated on achievement that it makes exhaustion inevitable. We've created what he terms "the achievement-subject": a person who is, in theory, free from external dominance but becomes dominated by internal pressure to achieve. "The achievement-subject," Han writes, "exploits itself until it burns out." The oppressor and the oppressed become the same person.

What's the alternative? Not laziness or indulgence, but a recovery of what the Slow Movement calls "tempo giusto"—the right pace, the appropriate rhythm. This isn't about doing nothing; it's about finding the natural cadence of human life, complete with variations in tempo, pauses between notes, and moments of rest that give meaning to moments of effort.

Tricia Hersey, founder of The Nap Ministry, frames rest not as an indulgence but as a form of resistance against systems that treat humans as mere production units. Her work began when, as a divinity student working multiple jobs, she noticed how exhaustion was affecting not just her wellbeing but her imagination and even her sense of hope. "Rest is resistance because it disrupts and pushes back against capitalism and white supremacy," she writes, connecting physical exhaustion to larger systems of exploitation. While her framing is political, the insight transcends ideology: when we refuse to rest, we collaborate in our own diminishment.

The biology of creativity also argues against constant productivity. Neuroscientists studying the creative process have identified the importance of what they call the "incubation phase"—periods when we step away from active problem-solving and allow our unconscious mind to make connections. This explains why insights often arrive during walks, showers, or just upon waking—moments when we're not actively trying to be productive. Forcing constant output paradoxically reduces our capacity for original thought.

A fascinating study from the University of Virginia highlighted how uncomfortable we've become with unproductive time. Researchers placed participants in a room with nothing to do but think for 15 minutes. They also gave them the option to administer a mild electric shock to themselves. Remarkably, 67% of men and 25% of women chose to shock themselves rather than sit quietly with their thoughts. We've become so averse to "doing nothing" that many of us would rather experience physical pain.

Our inability to be "useless" even affects how we treat illness. Swedish researcher Annemarie Mol has documented how contemporary culture forces sick people to maintain the performance of productivity. Rather than allowing illness to be a time of withdrawal and recovery, we expect the ill to "manage" their condition like a project, to "fight" their disease like a job. Even in our most vulnerable moments, the imperative to be useful never fully releases its grip.

Much of our resistance to non-productivity stems from a fundamental confusion about the nature of time. We tend to think of time as linear—a resource to be spent or saved like currency. But this mechanistic metaphor distorts the lived experience of time, which is more cyclical and variable. Some cultures recognize this more explicitly. The ancient Greeks distinguished between chronos (sequential, measured time) and kairos (the right or opportune moment). Our productivity obsession recognizes only chronos, missing the sensitivity to kairos—the understanding that not every moment is meant for the same kind of engagement.

The irony is that periods of apparent uselessness often prove profoundly useful in unexpected ways. A sabbatical that seems like an indulgence might prevent years of burnout. A day spent in nature with no tangible output might restore the very creativity that makes future work meaningful. A conversation that produces no action items might deepen a relationship that provides crucial support during a future crisis. The most "useful" thing you do this year might look, at first glance, completely useless.

The British psychoanalyst Donald Winnicott introduced the concept of "going-on-being"—the capacity to exist without reacting to external demands or internal pressure. He saw this state not as laziness but as a psychological achievement, a sign of health. People who cannot tolerate moments of non-productivity, he observed, often suffer from a fragile sense of self, requiring constant external validation through achievement. The capacity to simply be —to exist without constant doing—is actually a developmental milestone, not a regression.

Even animals instinctively understand the necessity of non-productive time. Lions sleep or rest up to 20 hours a day. Bears hibernate. Predators don't chase every prey they see; they conserve energy and hunt strategically. Yet we've convinced ourselves that constant activity is the natural state, when all evidence suggests it's profoundly unnatural.

A revealing study from Alex Soojung-Kim Pang, author of "Rest: Why You Get More Done When You Work Less," found that many of history's most productive creative figures worked intensely but briefly—typically no more than four or five hours per day. Charles Darwin took long daily walks. Mathematician Henri Poincaré worked in focused periods of two hours in the morning and two in the evening. Novelist Anthony Trollope wrote for three hours each morning before his day job at the postal service. Their significant contributions didn't come from working constantly but from working intensely and then stopping— allowing restoration, integration, and incubation.

The expectation of constant productivity particularly erodes activities that don't yield immediate, measurable outcomes. Deep friendship, philosophical reflection, appreciation of beauty, spiritual practice—these vital dimensions of human experience often appear "useless" by productivity metrics. Yet they're precisely what give life its texture and meaning beyond mere survival and accumulation.

Perhaps the most troubling aspect of our productivity obsession is how it reshapes our very identity. When usefulness becomes the core virtue, we begin to see ourselves primarily as functional units—valued for what we can produce rather than who we are. This transforms even our self-care into another form of work. We exercise not for joy but for longevity (to work more years). We meditate not for presence but for stress reduction (to work more efficiently). Even our rest becomes instrumental—not an inherent good but merely the means to more productivity.

The late philosopher Ivan Illich warned about this conflation of human value with economic utility. "We want to produce a new man, a man who is an efficient consumer of man-made products," he wrote. "This is the man whom our educational systems should produce." When education, healthcare, leisure, and even spirituality become oriented toward creating more productive workers rather than more complete humans, something essential is lost.

A woman named Eleanor Rigby (not the Beatles character but a real person with the same name) provides a poignant illustration of breaking free from the productivity trap. After decades in corporate finance working 70-hour weeks, she collapsed from exhaustion at age 42. During her recovery, her doctor prescribed something unusual: three months of "doing nothing productive." No self-improvement, no side projects, no planning her next career move. Just existing.

She describes the first two weeks as excruciating—filled with anxiety, guilt, and a profound identity crisis. But gradually, something shifted. Colors seemed more vivid. Conversations became less transactional. She found herself laughing more easily. "I realized I'd been holding my breath for twenty years," she later wrote. "I was experiencing life as a series of tasks to complete rather than moments to live." She didn't abandon work altogether—she eventually started a consulting practice—but with a fundamentally different relationship to productivity. It no longer defined her worth.

The path beyond productivity obsession isn't about abandoning meaningful work. It's about recognizing that human life naturally includes many modes of being: productive effort, yes, but also rest, play, contemplation, connection, and simple presence. None of these modes is inherently superior to the others. They form an ecology of experience, each necessary for the others to flourish.

What might this look like in practice? It starts with questioning the reflexive guilt we feel when we're not being "useful." It means creating deliberate spaces in life that have no productive purpose—time for wandering thoughts, aimless walks, conversation without agenda, or rest without justification. It means recognizing the different rhythms in our days, weeks, and years, and honoring them rather than flattening life into uniform productivity.

It also means examining our language. When we ask, "What did you do today?" we frame existence around activity. What if we sometimes asked instead, "What did you notice today?" or "What did you feel today?" or simply, "How was your being today?" These questions acknowledge dimensions of life beyond doing.

Most fundamentally, it requires remembering that humans are not machines, valued for their output. We are living beings whose worth is inherent, not earned through productivity. Our capacity for love, wisdom, beauty, and connection doesn't increase with our efficiency. Often, it depends on our willingness to be present in ways that appear, by conventional metrics, completely useless.

The 13th-century poet Rumi wrote: "There is a field beyond right doing and wrong doing. I'll meet you there." Perhaps there is also a field beyond useful doing and useless doing —beyond the very paradigm that measures life by its output. It's not a field we can produce or achieve or optimize our way into. We can only remember it's there, put down our tools for a while, and walk out to see who we might be when we're not being useful.

So the next time you find yourself apologizing for a day without achievement, or justifying rest as merely preparation for more work, or feeling guilty for moments of non-productivity—remember that you don't have to be useful all the time. Not because usefulness isn't valuable, but because it's only one note in the larger music of a human life. And sometimes the most important notes are the rests between—the caesuras, the pauses, the moments of silence that give meaning to everything else.

Conclusion: Maybe It's Not a Calling—Maybe It's Just a Life

We began this journey with a simple premise: that perhaps we've been asking the wrong question all along. "What should I do with my life?" has paralyzed more potential than it has unleashed. It assumes a singular answer exists, waiting to be discovered like buried treasure. It presupposes a linear path where passion leads to purpose leads to fulfillment—a neat narrative arc that rarely materializes in the messy business of actual living.

Fourteen essays later, I hope you've found not answers, but better questions. Not certainty, but comfort with ambiguity. Not a roadmap, but a compass.

The stories we tell about success and purpose often polish away the very details that make them instructive. Behind every "overnight success" lies a decade of false starts. Behind every "dream job" lies compromise and constraint. Behind every "perfect fit" lies adaptation and growth.

The anxiety of indecision feels uniquely personal when you're in it—as if everyone else somehow received clear instructions while you were left guessing. But this anxiety isn't a personal failing. It's the natural result of existing in a culture that simultaneously offers endless options while insisting that only a few of those options represent authentic living.

Researcher Bronnie Ware, who spent years working in palliative care, documented the most common regrets of the dying. High on that list was "I wish I'd had the courage to live a life true to myself, not the life others expected of me." But this insight is often misinterpreted as an endorsement of radical self-actualization—quitting everything to follow your passion. What the dying were actually lamenting wasn't their failure to pursue dramatic dreams, but their tendency to outsource their life choices to others' expectations. The regret wasn't about what they did, but about who they allowed to decide.

In the little-known novel "Stoner" by John Williams, the protagonist lives a seemingly unremarkable academic life, face-to-face with frequent disappointment and constraint. Yet the beauty of the book lies in how it reveals the quiet dignity of a life fully inhabited, even when that life doesn't match our cultural heroic narratives. Williams shows us that a life doesn't need to be extraordinary to be worth living—it simply needs to be authentically engaged with.

Throughout these essays, we've explored alternatives to the conventional wisdom that has left so many feeling inadequate. We've seen how the "follow your passion" mantra fails to account for how passion actually develops— through mastery rather than intuition. We've examined how treating life paths like a buffet rather than a soulmate liberates us from the paralysis of searching for the "one right thing." We've questioned whether work should be our primary identity at all and discovered how seemingly purposeless hobbies often become lifelines.

We've looked at how service to others can break decision paralysis faster than introspection, how embracing the generalist mindset opens doors that specialization keeps closed, and how sports teach us to value process over outcomes. We've dismantled the career ladder myth in favor of webs of connection, reframed restlessness as information rather than deficiency, and examined what becomes possible when we stop performing ambition for others' approval.

We've celebrated the radical act of being contentedly average at things we love, distinguished between inner and outer success metrics, advocated for small experiments over grand plans, and insisted that rest and play are not luxuries but necessities.

Now, as we reach the end, perhaps the most unconventional wisdom of all is this: maybe there is no calling. Maybe there's just life—a series of days to be lived with as much presence, curiosity, and kindness as we can muster.

The psychologist Abraham Maslow, famous for his hierarchy of needs and self-actualization theory, made a lesser-known but profound observation near the end of his life. He noted that his focus on the exceptional cases—self-actualized individuals—had perhaps missed something essential about ordinary goodness. In his later work, he became increasingly interested not in what makes people extraordinary, but in what makes everyday life meaningful.

The ancient Greeks distinguished between two concepts of time: chronos and kairos. Chronos represents sequential time—minutes, hours, days marching forward in linear progression. Kairos represents the right or opportune moment—times when something significant happens or could happen. A life rich in kairos isn't necessarily one filled with dramatic achievements, but one attentive to the moments that matter.

A few years ago, a massive study tracked thousands of graduates from elite universities to understand what factors predicted life satisfaction decades later. The researchers were surprised to discover that prestige, wealth, and conventional markers of success showed almost no correlation with well-being. What did correlate strongly? The quality of relationships, the experience of flow in daily activities, and the sense that one's work—whatever it was—contributed something worthwhile.

The truth is, most people don't find a singular purpose. They build a life—composite, evolving, and meaningful in its very incompleteness. They weave together various interests, relationships, and contributions. They learn to dance with uncertainty rather than defeat it. They find dignity not in arriving at final answers, but in asking better questions.

Modern life promises that somewhere out there is the perfect job, the perfect partner, the perfect house, the perfect lifestyle—if only we search hard enough, optimize diligently enough, hustle persistently enough. This promise has made us more anxious and less satisfied than previous generations who expected less perfection from their life choices.

The political philosopher Michael Sandel calls this "the tyranny of merit"—the belief that success is entirely a matter of individual choice and effort, which inevitably leads to a crushing sense of personal failure when reality doesn't match our aspirations. This mindset dismisses the role of luck, circumstance, and the simple fact that life isn't a meritocracy. Some of the most fulfilled people I know have made peace with the randomness of opportunity and outcome. They work hard not because they're guaranteed results, but because the work itself matters.

Drop the pressure. Not all at once—that's impossible in a world designed to keep us striving. But bit by bit, choice by choice. Question the narratives that tell you there's only one right way to live. Notice when you're making decisions to impress others versus decisions that align with your actual values. Pay attention to what activities make time disappear for you, what problems genuinely pique your curiosity.

The most liberating realization might be that you don't have to be exceptional to live a good life. You don't have to optimize every choice. You don't have to monetize every interest. You don't have to justify your existence through constant productivity.

A study from the Harvard Grant Study—one of the longest-running longitudinal studies of human development—followed participants for over 80 years to determine what factors lead to health and well-being. Their conclusion?

"Happiness is love. Full stop." Not achievement, not wealth, not even health itself, but the quality of human connections. The lead researcher, George Vaillant, put it this way: "Joy is connection...The more areas in your life you can make connection, the better."

There's a quiet dignity in figuring it out as you go—in embracing the experimental nature of a life rather than demanding certainty in advance. There's wisdom in understanding that meaning isn't something you find once and for all, but something you create and recreate through daily choices and attention.

Maybe your path won't make a neat story. Maybe it will zigzag and double back and occasionally disappear entirely. Maybe you'll never have that moment of perfect clarity where everything makes sense. Maybe that's not just okay, but exactly as it should be.

The poet Mary Oliver asked, "Tell me, what is it you plan to do with your one wild and precious life?" It's a beautiful question, but perhaps it puts too much pressure on having a plan. Perhaps the better question is: "How will you pay attention to your one wild and precious life as it unfolds?"

Because in the end, that might be all we can do—pay attention, stay curious, be kind, do work that feels worthwhile even when it's hard, rest when we need to, connect with others, and trust that meaning will emerge not from perfect choices but from how fully we inhabit the choices we make.

This isn't giving up on ambition. It's redefining it. Not as a destination to reach, but as a quality of engagement with whatever path you're on.

You don't need to know exactly what to do with your life. You just need to show up for it—day after day, choice after choice, with as much courage and consciousness as you can gather in each moment.

That's not settling. That's wisdom.

A Tiny Favor That Would Mean the World to Me

If you enjoyed this book and found it helpful, I would be truly grateful if you could take a moment to leave a review on Amazon.

It doesn't have to be long — even a few words make a huge difference.

Reviews help more people discover the book, and they let me know that the ideas inside have made an impact.

It would absolutely make my day to hear that something in these pages helped you, challenged you, or gave you a new way of seeing the world.

Thank you so much for reading — and for being part of this journey.

JM

My Next Book:

What To Do With Your Life...When You're 40 and Still Unsure

Here's a preview of my next title: introduction & first chapter of **What To Do With Your Life...***When You're 40 and Still Unsure.*

WHAT TO DO WITH YOUR LIFE

WHEN YOU ARE 40 AND STILL UNSURE

14 Unconventional Lessons

JAKE MORIMOTO

To be the first to know when it'll be released, you can subscribe to my newsletter here: self-improvement.me/wh
(and get 2 FREE bonuses!)

or just scan the QR code:

Introduction: You're Not Late —You're Just Not Lying

The most persistent lie of adulthood is that everyone else has figured it out.

Look around at your next dinner party, workplace meeting, or school pickup line. Behind the confident nods and assured statements about five-year plans, most people are improvising their way through existence with the same questions that keep you up at night. The difference isn't that they've found answers. It's that they've gotten comfortable pretending they have.

At forty, you've reached a curious threshold—old enough to see through the performance, young enough to change course. This peculiar intersection of wisdom and possibility doesn't represent failure. It represents the first moment in your life when you might actually be ready to tell yourself the truth.

The truth is messy. It whispers that perhaps you've been chasing someone else's definition of success. It suggests that certainty might be overrated. It dares to ask whether the path you've been following has your footprints on it, or just the imprints of expectations you've inherited.

Most of our culture treats midlife questioning as a crisis—an embarrassing breakdown of certainty that should be quickly resolved and never mentioned again. We're supposed to have it all figured out by thirty, executing flawlessly by forty. The narrative goes something like this: early twenties for exploration, late twenties for commitment, thirties for advancement, forties for peak achievement. By midlife, you should be harvesting the fruits of decisions made when you were practically still adolescent.

What a peculiar expectation.

The novelist George Eliot once observed, "It is never too late to be what you might have been." But I would go further: it's never too late to discover who you actually are. And forty isn't late—it might be right on time.

Carl Jung, the Swiss psychiatrist whose work on personal development still resonates a century later, spoke of life as having two halves. The first half, roughly until midlife, involves establishing yourself in the world—career, family, social position. The second half is about meaning, integration, and individuation. Jung believed most people make the mistake of carrying the goals and strategies of life's first half into its second half, where they no longer serve.

In other words, what got you here won't get you there.

The pressure to have life "figured out" by forty stems from a fundamental misunderstanding of human development. We are not finished products by midlife; we are works in progress until our final breath. Psychologist Laura Carstensen at Stanford University has found through her research that emotional intelligence actually increases with age, alongside our ability to regulate emotions and prioritize meaningful experiences. The neuroplasticity of our brains—their ability to form new connections and pathways—continues throughout life. We remain capable of profound change, adaptation, and discovery at forty, fifty, sixty, and beyond.

Perhaps you've felt the subtle shame of not having arrived at some imaginary destination by now. A voice that says everyone else is content with their choices, fulfilled in their purpose, secure in their identity. Let me offer an alternative interpretation: you're not behind. You're just awake.

David Epstein, in his groundbreaking book "Range," chronicles how some of the world's most successful people take longer, more circuitous routes to finding their ultimate contribution. He challenges the "10,000 hours of deliberate practice" narrative by demonstrating how breadth of experience—sometimes appearing as indecision or career meandering—often leads to more innovative, satisfying work. The person who has tried many paths brings a richer perspective to whatever they ultimately do.

Remember filmmaker Ava DuVernay? She didn't pick up a camera until age 32, after a successful career in publicity. Her "late" entry into filmmaking didn't hinder her—it informed her unique perspective and approach. By 45, she had become the first Black female director to helm a $100 million film.

The intimidating thing about forty isn't the number. It's the growing suspicion that you can no longer blame circumstances, timing, or other people for the gap between the life you have and the life you want. It's the dawning realization that if something is going to change, you'll have to change it.

This realization isn't a crisis. It's an invitation.

Throughout my conversations with people navigating midlife transitions, I've noticed something striking: those who find their way through aren't necessarily the ones with the most resources, connections, or even clarity. They're the ones willing to question everything while still moving forward. They practice what investor Charlie Munger calls "worldly wisdom"—the ability to draw connections between disciplines and see patterns where others see chaos.

A former banking executive told me about the moment he realized he'd spent twenty years solving problems he didn't care about. "I wasn't failed by my career," he said. "I failed to notice I had outgrown it." At 44, he left to start a financial literacy program for teenagers in underserved communities. The work pays less but demands more of him —his creativity, his empathy, his full presence. "For the first time," he said, "I'm not just using my skills. I'm using myself."

His story illustrates a crucial point: confusion at forty doesn't mean you've done something wrong. It might mean you've done something right—you've remained honest enough with yourself to notice when the life you've built no longer fits the person you've become.

The essays that follow aren't about dramatic reinvention or finding the "perfect" answer to the question of what to do with your life. They're about something more fundamental: learning to ask better questions. Questions that cut through cultural conditioning about success, purpose, and fulfillment. Questions that honor the complexity of a human life at midpoint. Questions that create space for possibility rather than collapse it into premature certainty.

These questions matter because by forty, you've lived long enough to know that genuine fulfillment rarely comes from external markers. The promotion, the bigger house, the impressive title—these things shimmer with promise until they're achieved, then quickly become the new normal. Psychologists call this the "hedonic treadmill"—our tendency to quickly return to a relatively stable level of happiness despite major positive or negative events.

So if external achievements won't sustain us, what will? The research points consistently toward a few factors: meaningful work, deep relationships, autonomy, mastery, contribution to others, and alignment between our values and our daily lives. Notice that none of these require a particular career path, income level, or social status. They're available through countless configurations of life choices.

The psychologist Marsha Linehan observes that "the path to wisdom lies in the ability to hold opposing truths at once." At forty, you've earned the right to embrace contradiction: You can be both proud of what you've built and ready to tear it down. You can honor your past choices while making different ones now. You can acknowledge your limitations while expanding your possibilities.

A former client—a successful architect who felt increasingly alienated from her work—described her midlife questioning this way: "It's like I've been speaking a language fluently for twenty years, only to realize it's not my native tongue." At 47, she scaled back her practice to pursue a degree in environmental science. "People thought I was having a breakdown," she laughed. "But actually, I was having a breakthrough."

The essays ahead will challenge conventional wisdom about careers, purpose, identity, and what constitutes a well-lived life. They'll question the persistent American mythology that says we must constantly strive, achieve, and optimize. They'll suggest that perhaps the best parts of you are not the most productive or impressive parts. They'll propose that confusion might be a more honest response to life's complexity than certainty ever could be.

This book won't offer ten steps to clarity or promise that by the final page, you'll have a master plan for the rest of your days. Such promises would undermine the central argument here: that a meaningful life emerges not from having all the answers, but from asking better questions and staying awake to their unfolding answers.

What you'll find instead are invitations to think differently about this rich, complex season of life. To see your uncertainty not as a problem to solve but as perception finally clear enough to notice the cracks in simplistic narratives about success and fulfillment. To recognize that in a culture obsessed with knowing, there is radical power in admitting: "I'm still figuring it out."

Because the truth is, we all are. Some of us just stopped saying it out loud.

You're not late. You're not lost. You're just not lying anymore—not to yourself, not to others. And in that honesty, everything becomes possible again.

1 - The Success You Wanted Then Might Be the Trap Now

There's a peculiar alchemy that happens around age forty. The gold you once chased—that bright, shiny success you mapped out in your twenties—can suddenly feel like lead in your hands. Heavy. Constraining. Not at all what you thought it would be.

We don't talk about this enough. How the victory lap can feel like a prison yard. How the corner office with the view can become a gilded cage. How the success that consumed your youth might be the very thing suffocating you now.

This isn't about ingratitude. It's about honesty.

When I encounter people at midlife crossroads, the conversation almost always circles back to the same revelation: "I got what I wanted. And now I'm not sure I want it anymore." There's usually a pause after this confession, as if they've uttered something shameful. As if changing your mind about your life's direction is some sort of moral failing.

It isn't.

The dream job you landed at twenty-eight was chosen by a different version of you—someone with different values, different knowledge, and different priorities. You were making decisions with partial information, not just about the world, but about yourself. The psychological phenomenon known as the "end of history illusion" explains this perfectly. Coined by researchers Daniel Gilbert and Jordi Quoidbach, it describes our tendency to believe we've finished changing—that the person we are today is the person we'll be forever. Their studies showed that people consistently underestimate how much they'll change in the future, despite acknowledging how much they've changed in the past.

At twenty-five, you couldn't possibly know what forty would feel like. You were guessing, at best.

The story of Roger Horchow isn't widely known outside business circles, but it beautifully illustrates this turning point. Horchow built a luxury mail-order catalog empire that made him wealthy and respected. By conventional metrics, he'd "made it." Then at forty-something, he sold the company. Colleagues were baffled. Why walk away from such success? Because Horchow realized the business had become more about maintenance than meaning. He shifted to Broadway producing, helping create shows like "Crazy for You," finding a creative outlet that reawakened something in him. He didn't reject success—he redefined it.

The success you want at forty isn't always visual, measurable, or LinkedIn-friendly. It's often internal, textured, and impossible to capture in a résumé bullet point.

We cling to old definitions of success like life rafts, even when they're sinking us. The lawyer who hates practicing law but can't let go of the prestige. The executive who fantasizes about teaching but won't surrender the status.

The doctor who dreams of writing novels but can't abandon the identity she's spent decades building. The trap isn't the career itself—it's the death grip on a declining dream.

Harvard psychologist Daniel Gilbert's research on "affective forecasting" adds another layer to this dilemma. His studies demonstrate that humans are remarkably poor at predicting what will make them happy in the future. We consistently misjudge how long and intensely we'll feel emotions in response to both good and bad events. The promotion you once believed would bring lasting fulfillment likely delivered a shorter happiness boost than you anticipated. The failures you feared would devastate you probably didn't crush you for as long as you expected.

This isn't just academic theory—it's the explanation for that nagging sense of "is this it?" that haunts many successful forty-somethings.

A few years ago, I encountered a woman at a conference—let's call her Elaine. At forty-three, she had the legal career she'd plotted since high school: partner at a prestigious firm, respected in her field, financially secure. She also had a secret: she was profoundly unhappy. What began as private journaling about her dissatisfaction eventually led her to take a three-month sabbatical to work with a wildlife conservation project. Against every practical consideration, this corporate attorney found herself tracking endangered species through remote forests.

"I thought I was having a breakdown," she told me over coffee. "Then I realized I was having a breakthrough."

Elaine never returned to legal practice. She now works as a legal advisor for environmental organizations—making less money but feeling engaged in a way she hadn't for decades. The success she had achieved wasn't wrong; it just wasn't right anymore.

This pattern repeats endlessly across professions and personalities. The architect who realizes she wants to teach elementary school. The finance professional who dreams of running a small farm. The marketing executive who longs to become a therapist. These aren't failures of commitment or character. They're evidence of growth.

At forty, you're experiencing what psychologist Carol Gilligan might call an "integration crisis"—a necessary disruption where competing parts of yourself demand reconciliation. The ambitious competitor meets the person who craves meaning. The security-seeker confronts the risk-taker. The professional identity collides with other aspects of selfhood that have been lying dormant.

The trap tightens when we interpret these conflicts as weakness rather than wisdom.

Most self-help narratives around midlife focus on "finding your passion" or "reinventing yourself," as if you need to discard everything and start from zero. This misses the point. The challenge isn't to erase your past or reject your achievements. It's to recognize that the success template you've been following may have reached its expiration date.

Psychologist James Hollis speaks of the "second adulthood" that begins in midlife—a phase where the governing question shifts from "What does the world want from me?" to "What does the soul want from me?" This isn't mystical jargon. It's about moving from external validation to internal alignment.

The success that once motivated you likely came with scripts: If I achieve X, I'll be respected. If I earn Y, I'll be secure. If I reach position Z, I'll be fulfilled. These equations seemed reliable in your twenties and thirties. By forty, you've run the calculations enough times to know they don't always balance.

This realization can feel like failure. It's not. It's clarity.

A lesser-known study from the Harvard Business Review found that professionals who make significant career shifts in their forties often report higher satisfaction than those who stay on linear paths—not despite the disruption, but because of it. The research suggested that it wasn't the specific new direction that mattered most, but the act of choosing consciously rather than continuing through momentum.

Former NFL player John Urschel offers a compelling illustration of letting go of a successful path that no longer fits. As a Baltimore Ravens offensive lineman, Urschel achieved what countless young athletes dream of. Yet at twenty-six, he walked away from football at the height of his career to pursue mathematics. While technically younger than forty, his story captures the essence of recognizing when continued success in one arena might constrain your growth in another.

"I no longer wish to risk my health for a game," Urschel explained when he retired. But the deeper motivation was positive, not negative. His passion for mathematical research had grown to the point where football—despite its prestige and financial rewards—felt like a distraction from what truly engaged him.

Today, Urschel is completing a PhD in mathematics at MIT. The success he wanted then became the trap he needed to escape.

This isn't just about career. Success traps appear in every domain. The marriage that once felt like an achievement but now feels like an arrangement. The social circle that once validated you but now constrains you. The lifestyle that impressed others but never quite satisfied you.

At forty, these dissonances become harder to ignore.

What makes these transitions so challenging isn't necessarily the practical considerations, though those are real. It's the identity crisis that accompanies them. After decades of introducing yourself as a lawyer, doctor, executive, or expert, who are you if you step away from that role? When you've built a life around certain metrics of success, what happens when you change the measurements?

The writer David Foster Wallace captured this predicament perfectly: "The really important kind of freedom involves attention, and awareness, and discipline, and effort, and being able truly to care about other people and to sacrifice for them, over and over, in myriad petty little unsexy ways, every day." The freedom to redefine success at forty isn't about abandoning responsibility—it's about recommitting to what genuinely matters.

Sometimes the trap isn't even of your own making. Cultural narratives about "having it all" or "living your best life" create impossible standards that turn even objective successes into perceived failures. Social media amplifies this, presenting curated versions of others' lives against which you measure your messy reality.

By forty, you're experienced enough to see through these illusions, but that doesn't automatically free you from their influence.

Breaking free requires something counterintuitive: gratitude for the very success that now constrains you. That career provided security, skills, and experiences that make your current awareness possible. That relationship taught you about love, even if it's ending. That achievement opened doors, even if you're now walking through different ones.

The success wasn't wrong. It just served its purpose.

There's a wonderful concept in ecology called "succession"—how ecosystems naturally evolve through different stages, each one necessary for the next to emerge. What worked perfectly in one phase becomes limiting in another. The pioneering species that thrive after a forest fire create conditions that eventually make way for different plants. Nothing has failed; everything has served.

Your earlier success is like those pioneer species. It created conditions for something new to grow.

At forty, you have resources your younger self lacked: perspective, financial stability (maybe), self-knowledge, professional skills, and networks. The success that now feels constraining has given you tools to build something different.

What would happen if you saw your current dissatisfaction not as a midlife crisis but as midlife clarity? Not as failure but as graduation?

The trap loosens when you recognize that succeeding at something doesn't obligate you to do it forever. The trap breaks when you realize that changing direction isn't betrayal—it's growth.

There's a remarkable liberation in acknowledging that the success you wanted then might be the trap now. It creates space to ask better questions: What would success look like if I defined it today, from scratch? What felt like success when I wasn't looking? What kinds of accomplishment give me energy rather than depleting it?

The answers might surprise you. They might lead to dramatic external changes, or they might transform how you experience your existing life. They might redefine success entirely.

At forty, you don't need a new five-year plan. You need permission to question the plans that brought you here. You need the courage to acknowledge when yesterday's definition of success has become today's constraint.

The path forward isn't about abandonment. It's about integration. How can the skills, resources, and wisdom from your first-act success serve what calls to you now? How can you honor what was while creating what could be?

There's no universal playbook for this transition. Some people make radical external changes: new careers, relationships, locations. Others transform from within, bringing fresh energy and perspective to existing circumstances. The common thread isn't what changes, but the willingness to question yesterday's success template.

The success you wanted then might be the trap now. But here's the beautiful paradox: recognizing the trap is itself a form of success—perhaps the most meaningful kind. It means you're awake enough to notice the dissonance, brave enough to acknowledge it, and alive enough to do something about it.

That's not a midlife crisis. That's midlife courage.

Subscribe to my newsletter to know when the book will be out (I only email about books):

self-improvement.me/wh

My Other Books

How To Become Smarter: 14 Unconventional Lessons To Elevate Your Life Choices, Career and Confidence

Available on Amazon for FREE (Kindle version)

How To Be Respected: 14 Unconventional Lessons on How You Earn Respect—and Keep It

Available on Amazon

Subscribe to my newsletter to know when my next books will be out (I only email about books):

self-improvement.me/wh

Acknowledgments

This book would not exist without the generous minds and hearts who helped shape it.

To Melissa and Paul, my incredibly talented editors—thank you for once again challenging every lazy idea, sharpening every lesson, and believing in this project when, just like all others, it was still just a mess of random notes.

To my family, who (I know I keep & keep saying this) never stopped believing in me, even when I had stopped believing in myself—thank you for your unwavering love and patience.

And to all the thinkers, writers, athletes, artists, and rebels —known and unknown—whose unconventional wisdom lit the path: this book is a thank-you letter in essay form.

About The Author

Jake Morimoto has been writing quietly for years. A lifelong notetaker and lover of contrarian ideas, he finally decided to share his work with the world. *Think Against* is his publishing debut—a sharp, distilled manifesto for those who think sideways. He lives simply, writes daily, and prefers questions to answers.

Bibliography

INTRODUCTION

Botton, A. de. (2009). *The Pleasures and Sorrows of Work*. Pantheon Books.

Csikszentmihalyi, M. (1997). *Creativity: Flow and the Psychology of Discovery and Invention*. Harper Perennial.

Munger, C. T. (1995). *The Psychology of Human Misjudgment*. Speech at Harvard University.

Newport, C. (2012). *So Good They Can't Ignore You: Why Skills Trump Passion in the Quest for Work You Love*. Grand Central Publishing.

Oettingen, G. (2014). *Rethinking Positive Thinking: Inside the New Science of Motivation*. Current.

Sivers, D. (2011). *Anything You Want: 40 Lessons for a New Kind of Entrepreneur*. Portfolio.

CHAPTER 1

Csikszentmihalyi, M. (1990). *Flow: The Psychology of Optimal Experience*. Harper & Row.

Duckworth, A. (2016). *Grit: The Power of Passion and Perseverance*. Scribner.

Grant, A. (2019). "The Career Advice You Probably Didn't Get." Harvard Business Review.

Murakami, H. (2007). What I Talk About When I Talk About Running. Knopf.

Newport, C. (2012). So Good They Can't Ignore You: Why Skills Trump Passion in the Quest for Work You Love. Grand Central Publishing.

Omidyar, P. (2002). "How I Did It: Pierre Omidyar on Creating eBay." Harvard Business Review.

Rowe, M. (2016). Profoundly Disconnected: A True Confession From Mike Rowe. Rowe Foundation Press.

Thiel, P. (2014). Zero to One: Notes on Startups, or How to Build the Future. Crown Business.

CHAPTER 2

Burnett, B., & Evans, D. (2016). *Designing Your Life: How to Build a Well-Lived, Joyful Life*. Knopf.

Dweck, C. (2006). *Mindset: The New Psychology of Success*. Random House.

Epstein, D. (2019). *Range: Why Generalists Triumph in a Specialized World*. Riverhead Books.

Gilbert, D. (2006). *Stumbling on Happiness*. Knopf.

Ibarra, H. (2003). *Working Identity: Unconventional Strategies for Reinventing Your Career*. Harvard Business School Press.

Krumboltz, J. (2009). *The Happenstance Learning Theory*. Journal of Career Assessment, 17(2), 135-154.

McAdams, D. (2001). *The Psychology of Life Stories*. Review of General Psychology, 5(2), 100-122.

Schwartz, B. (2004). *The Paradox of Choice: Why More Is Less*. Ecco.

Seligman, M. E. P. (2011). *Flourish: A Visionary New Understanding of Happiness and Well-being*. Free Press.

Vaillant, G. (2012). *Triumphs of Experience: The Men of the Harvard Grant Study*. Harvard University Press.

CHAPTER 3

Crawford, Matthew B. *Shop Class as Soulcraft: An Inquiry into the Value of Work*. Penguin Books, 2010.

Dillard, Annie. "Write Till You Drop." *The New York Times*, May 28, 1989.

Han, Byung-Chul. *The Burnout Society*. Stanford University Press, 2015.

Kittay, Eva Feder. *Love's Labor: Essays on Women, Equality, and Dependency*. Routledge, 1999.

Krznaric, Roman. *How to Find Fulfilling Work*. Picador, 2013.

Lazarsfeld, Paul. *The Unemployed Man and His Family*. Dryden Press, 1940.

Sennett, Richard. *The Craftsman*. Yale University Press, 2009.

Weber, Max. *The Protestant Ethic and the Spirit of Capitalism*. Routledge, 2001.

CHAPTER 4

Bateson, M. C. (1990). *Composing a Life*. Plume.

Child, J. (2006). *My Life in France*. Knopf.

Csikszentmihalyi, M. (1990). *Flow: The Psychology of Optimal Experience*. Harper & Row.

Feynman, R. P. (1985). *"Surely You're Joking, Mr. Feynman!": Adventures of a Curious Character*. W. W. Norton & Company.

Gendlin, E. T. (1982). *Focusing*. Bantam.

Hyde, L. (1983). *The Gift: Imagination and the Erotic Life of Property*. Vintage Books.

O'Donohue, J. (1997). *Anam Cara: A Book of Celtic Wisdom*. Harper Collins.

Torvalds, L. & Diamond, D. (2001). *Just for Fun: The Story of an Accidental Revolutionary*. HarperBusiness.

Winnicott, D. W. (1971). *Playing and Reality*. Tavistock Publications.

CHAPTER 5

Buber, M. (1923). I and Thou. Charles Scribner's Sons.

Emory University Department of Psychiatry and Behavioral Sciences. (2016). The Neuroscience of Giving. Journal of Happiness Studies.

Kornfield, J. (1993). A Path with Heart: A Guide Through the Perils and Promises of Spiritual Life. Bantam Books.

LinkedIn Corporation. (2018). Volunteer Experience Survey: Impact on Hiring Decisions. LinkedIn Talent Solutions.

Thurman, H. (1980). With Head and Heart: The Autobiography of Howard Thurman. Harcourt Brace Jovanovich.

Yamada, H. (2013). Fukushima's Gray Army: Retirement and Renewal After Disaster. The Japan Times.

CHAPTER 6

de Botton, A. (2009). *The Pleasures and Sorrows of Work*. Pantheon Books.

Epstein, D. (2019). *Range: Why Generalists Triumph in a Specialized World*. Riverhead Books.

Kerrigan, A. (2021). *Sensory Design: Creating Spaces for Extraordinary Minds*. Echo Press.

Munger, C. (2005). *Poor Charlie's Almanack: The Wit and Wisdom of Charles T. Munger*. Walsworth Publishing Company.

Newport, C. (2012). *So Good They Can't Ignore You: Why Skills Trump Passion in the Quest for Work You Love.* Grand Central Publishing.

Twain, M. (1894). *Pudd'nhead Wilson.* American Publishing Company.

CHAPTER 7

Csikszentmihalyi, M. (1990). Flow: The Psychology of Optimal Experience. Harper & Row.

Duckworth, A. (2016). Grit: The Power of Passion and Perseverance. Scribner.

Holiday, R. (2014). The Obstacle Is the Way: The Timeless Art of Turning Trials into Triumph. Portfolio.

Jones, L. (2015). Body Lengths. Black Inc.

Kübler-Ross, E. (1969). On Death and Dying. Macmillan.

Redmond, D. (2000). Inspirational Olympians. Oxford University Press.

Seneca. (2005). On the Shortness of Life. Penguin Classics.

Taleb, N. N. (2012). Antifragile: Things That Gain from Disorder. Random House.

Torres, D. (2009). Age is Just a Number: Achieve Your Dreams at Any Stage in Your Life. Broadway Books.

CHAPTER 8

Arthur, W. B. (1996). Increasing Returns and the New World of Business. Harvard Business Review, 74(4), 100-109.

Burke, J. (1978). Connections. Little Brown & Co.

Epstein, D. (2019). Range: Why Generalists Triumph in a Specialized World. Riverhead Books.

Newport, C. (2016). Deep Work: Rules for Focused Success in a Distracted World. Grand Central Publishing.

Tett, G. (2015). The Silo Effect: The Peril of Expertise and the Promise of Breaking Down Barriers. Simon & Schuster.

Torvalds, L., & Diamond, D. (2001). Just for Fun: The Story of an Accidental Revolutionary. HarperBusiness.

Walker, K. (2017). Kara Walker: The Ecstasy of St. Kara. Yale University Press.

CHAPTER 9

Ariely, Dan. *Predictably Irrational: The Hidden Forces That Shape Our Decisions.* HarperCollins, 2008.

Csikszentmihalyi, Mihaly. *Flow: The Psychology of Optimal Experience.* Harper & Row, 1990.

Doctorow, E.L. *The Paris Review*, "The Art of Fiction No. 94," Winter 1986.

Levitin, Daniel J. *The Organized Mind: Thinking Straight in the Age of Information Overload.* Dutton, 2014.

Lindbergh, Anne Morrow. *Gift from the Sea.* Pantheon Books, 1955.

Newport, Cal. *So Good They Can't Ignore You: Why Skills Trump Passion in the Quest for Work You Love*. Business Plus, 2012.

Thaler, Richard H. and Cass R. Sunstein. *Nudge: Improving Decisions About Health, Wealth, and Happiness*. Yale University Press, 2008.

CHAPTER 10

Csikszentmihalyi, Mihaly. *Flow: The Psychology of Optimal Experience*. Harper & Row, 1990.

Goffman, Erving. *The Presentation of Self in Everyday Life*. Anchor Books, 1959.

Heidegger, Martin. *Being and Time*. Harper Perennial Modern Classics, 2008.

Jung, Carl Gustav. *The Undiscovered Self*. New American Library, 2006.

Lévi-Strauss, Claude. *Myth and Meaning*. Routledge, 2001.

Miller, Alice. *The Drama of the Gifted Child*. Basic Books, 2008.

Newport, Cal. *So Good They Can't Ignore You: Why Skills Trump Passion in the Quest for Work You Love*. Grand Central Publishing, 2012.

Spolin, Viola. *Improvisation for the Theater*. Northwestern University Press, 1999.

Winnicott, D.W. *Playing and Reality*. Routledge, 2005.

CHAPTER 11

Buechner, Frederick. *Wishful Thinking: A Theological ABC*. Harper & Row, 1973.

Csikszentmihalyi, Mihaly. *Flow: The Psychology of Optimal Experience*. Harper & Row, 1990.

Damon, Young. *The Art of Reading*. Melbourne University Publishing, 2016.

Johnson, Steven. *Where Good Ideas Come From: The Natural History of Innovation*. Riverhead Books, 2010.

Oakley, Barbara. *A Mind for Numbers: How to Excel at Math and Science*. TarcherPerigee, 2014.

Rodriguez, Tori. "Negative Effects of Digital Health Tracking," *Scientific American Mind*, 28(2), 2017.

Seligman, Martin. *Flourish: A Visionary New Understanding of Happiness and Well-being*. Free Press, 2011.

University of Michigan. "Recreational Pursuits and Subjective Well-being," *Journal of Leisure Research*, 51(4), 2019.

Vonnegut, Kurt. *A Man Without a Country*. Seven Stories Press, 2005.

Winnicott, Donald W. *The Child, the Family, and the Outside World*. Penguin Books, 1964.

CHAPTER 12

Buffett, W. (1991). *The Warren Buffett Way: Investment Strategies of the World's Greatest Investor*. Wiley.

Csikszentmihalyi, M. (1990). *Flow: The Psychology of Optimal Experience*. Harper & Row.

Fermor, P. L. (1977). *A Time of Gifts*. John Murray.

Harris, S. (2014). *Waking Up: A Guide to Spirituality Without Religion*. Simon & Schuster.

Kasser, T., & Ryan, R. M. (1996). "Further examining the American dream: Differential correlates of intrinsic and extrinsic goals." *Personality and Social Psychology Bulletin*, 22, 280-287.

Munger, C. (2008). *Poor Charlie's Almanack: The Wit and Wisdom of Charles T. Munger*. Donning Company Publishers.

Van Ronk, D. (2005). *The Mayor of MacDougal Street: A Memoir*. Da Capo Press.

CHAPTER 13

Frazier, I. (1989). *The Conversationalist*. Farrar, Straus and Giroux.

Gadsby, H. (2018). *Nanette*. Netflix.

Mullen, R. (2004). *The Mutt: How to Skateboard and Not Kill Yourself*. ReganBooks.

Sims, P. (2011). *Little Bets: How Breakthrough Ideas Emerge from Small Discoveries*. Free Press.

Terman, L. M. (1959). *The Gifted Group at Mid-Life: Thirty-Five Years' Follow-Up of the Superior Child.* Stanford University Press.

Thiel, P. (2014). *Zero to One: Notes on Startups, or How to Build the Future.* Crown Business.

Wooden, J. (1997). *Wooden: A Lifetime of Observations and Reflections On and Off the Court.* Contemporary Books.

CHAPTER 14

Han, B. C. (2015). *The Burnout Society.* Stanford University Press.

Hersey, T. (2022). *Rest Is Resistance: A Manifesto.* Little, Brown Spark.

Hunnicutt, B. (2013). *Free Time: The Forgotten American Dream.* Temple University Press.

Illich, I. (1971). *Deschooling Society.* Harper & Row.

Mol, A. (2008). *The Logic of Care: Health and the Problem of Patient Choice.* Routledge.

Pang, A. S. K. (2016). *Rest: Why You Get More Done When You Work Less.* Basic Books.

Whyte, D. (2002). *The Heart Aroused: Poetry and the Preservation of the Soul in Corporate America.* Currency Doubleday.

Wilson, T. D., Reinhard, D. A., Westgate, E. C., Gilbert, D. T., Ellerbeck, N., Hahn, C., Brown, C. L., & Shaked, A.

(2014). "Just think: The challenges of the disengaged mind." *Science*, 345(6192), 75-77.

Winnicott, D. W. (1960). "The Theory of the Parent-Infant Relationship." *International Journal of Psycho-Analysis*, 41, 585-595.

CONCLUSION

Grant, K., & Sandberg, S. (2013). *Option B: Facing Adversity, Building Resilience, and Finding Joy*. Knopf.

Oliver, M. (1992). *New and Selected Poems, Volume One*. Beacon Press.

Sandel, M. J. (2020). *The Tyranny of Merit: What's Become of the Common Good?*. Farrar, Straus and Giroux.

Vaillant, G. E. (2012). *Triumphs of Experience: The Men of the Harvard Grant Study*. Harvard University Press.

Ware, B. (2012). *The Top Five Regrets of the Dying: A Life Transformed by the Dearly Departing*. Hay House.

Williams, J. (1965). *Stoner*. Viking Press.